D1709831

FARMACY KITCHEN

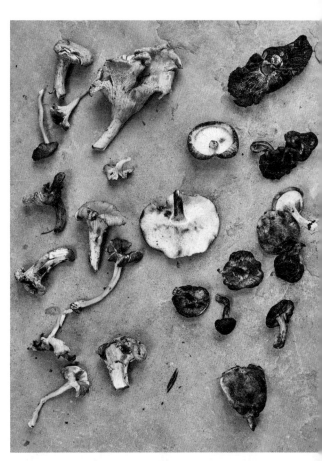

Plant-based recipes for a conscious way of life

FARMACY KITCHEN

Created by
Camilla Fayed with Susie Pearl,
Emily Pearson and Pietro Cuevas

aster

For my Nana, Anisa Martinson, a talented Finnish oil painter whose love
for cooking and flavor has inspired my culinary journey. Your eternally
grateful Granddaughter.

An Hachette UK Company
www.hachette.co.uk

First published in Great Britain in 2018 by Aster, a division of Octopus Publishing
Group Ltd, Carmelite House, 50 Victoria Embankment, London EC4Y 0DZ
www.octopusbooks.co.uk

Distributed in the US by Hachette Book Group, 1290 Avenue of the Americas,
4th and 5th Floors, New York, NY 10104

Distributed in Canada by Canadian Manda Group, 664 Annette St., Toronto,
Ontario, Canada M6S 2C8

ISBN 978-1-91202-346-2

A CIP catalog record for this book is available from the
British Library.

Printed and bound in China

10 9 8 7 6 5 4 3 2 1

Consultant Publisher: Kate Adams
Senior Editor: Pollyanna Poulter
Copy Editor: Mary-Jane Wilkins
Art Director: Juliette Norsworthy
Photographer: Nick Hopper
Illustrator: Ella Mclean
Home Economist and Food Stylist: Sian Henley
Prop Stylist: Linda Berlin
Production Manager: Caroline Alberti

Nutritional info
recipe codes

✳
GF = gluten free

✳
NF = nut free

✳
R = raw

✳
VG = vegan

Contents

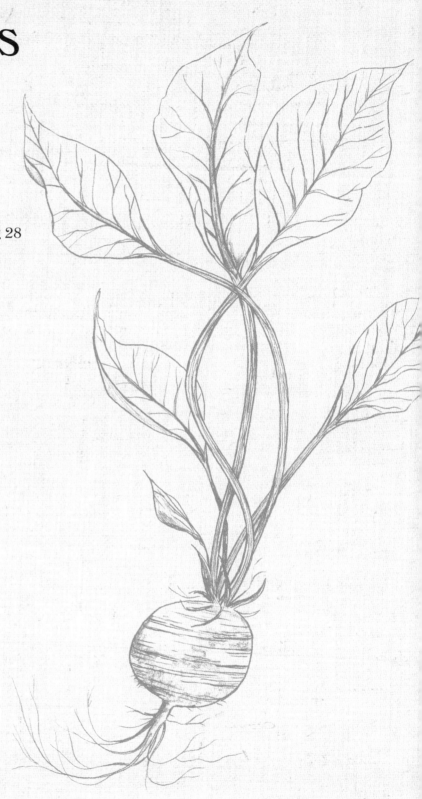

Foreword

Welcome to the Farmacy Kitchen where you will find inspirational ideas for conscious living and delicious recipes for plant-based eating that support both vegan and vegetarian diets. The Farmacy ethos aims to bring our attention back to nature, simplicity, and balance. We love to follow the concept of "simple abundance" in the food we create, using fresh, colorful wholefoods in inspired combinations for maximum flavor as well as easy digestion and enjoyment.

Farmacy London opened its doors in Notting Hill in 2016. The restaurant's mission is to offer a range of fresh, seasonal, and nutritionally balanced plant-based food sourced from local, sustainable, and environmentally conscious suppliers.

Life gets busy and it's often hard to find time to cook well at home and to balance the need for nutrition and flavor in our daily diet while avoiding processed food, sugar, and animal products. Farmacy helps you create this balance.

We know how good food tastes when it's made with love and intention. Cooking is a creative process and this books shows you how to make great-tasting food to nourish the body and energize the soul—a process you can bring to your own kitchen.

It's becoming more important than ever to think about the way we choose to eat and live, and the impact modern living is having on us, our planet, and its natural resources. In this book you'll find new and helpful ideas on cooking well with plant-based food and how to make some important changes that will make a difference. We look at how a conscious way of living not only benefits individual health, but also communities, the environment, and the world in general.

There is a list of essentials for your kitchen so that you have everything ready to cook well and we look at the best ways to bring in sustainable and affordable practices at home. Here is a collection of recipes that are straightforward whatever your level of cooking expertise. We are not trying to convert anyone. These are recipes that can be easily introduced to your diet and you don't have to be vegetarian to enjoy them.

I've been passionate about food since I was very young, but I haven't always eaten healthily. It has been a long journey for me, with many challenges, to enjoy eating a healthy, plant-based diet. The food I was eating in my teenage years and early twenties consisted largely of junk food. I ate a lot of processed food and regularly drank alcohol to be sociable. I put on weight, felt low in energy, and had high cholesterol and other health issues as a result of poor nutrition. I was due for a wake-up call.

When I started a family, I realized that I had no choice but to put health and well-being at the top of my list of priorities. Being pregnant, I had to make some changes to the way I was choosing to live and eat. I knew that changing my diet and lifestyle could have a huge impact on how I felt on a physical level. The surprise was how it made me feel emotionally.

I was lucky to be able to travel to different places around the world to find out about new ways of eating and living.

I feel passionate about sharing this widely, passing on the information that I've learned. My interest in growing food and biodynamic gardening increases as I find out more about the importance of where food comes from.

On this journey to healthier living, I've met some amazing people who have taught me so much. My thanks extend to all the teachers who have helped along the way and set me on this journey. I am filled with appreciation for those who pushed me to keep going when the mountain seemed too high to climb. This is an exciting time, when many people are coming together to enjoy plant-based eating with a shared intention to make better choices and live a healthier life.

Enjoy!
With love

Camilla

Nature knows best when it comes to food, health, and balance. Our approach is to create food that is delicious, and good for the body and the Earth.

Farmacy Philosophy

An introduction

The world is waking up to the benefits of eating fresh, local ingredients that are grown and produced without harmful pesticides and without harm to animals. There is a strong shift in global consciousness with many people looking for more connection, kindness, and compassion in life.

The recipes in this book use wholefoods, making good-tasting food that is naturally high in nutrients. At Farmacy we avoid processed ingredients and choose organic whenever possible to avoid ingesting the chemicals and pesticides used in nonorganic food production. We do not use canned food or food that is clearly "dead," instead opting for fresh and living food that is well sourced. Our recipes avoid using ingredients that can be high in genetically modified organisms (GMOs) such as corn, soy, potatoes, and wheat.

In this chapter we outline our food philosophy and lay out the benefits of conscious eating—it makes a real difference. When we eat with awareness, the food tastes better somehow, we feel we are nourished in a deeper way, and our bodies digest more completely when we bring awareness to the process of eating. It is true that often this way of eating and living is considered a luxury, but more people than ever are becoming aware of their choices around food, and conscious eating is becoming a familiar part of life.

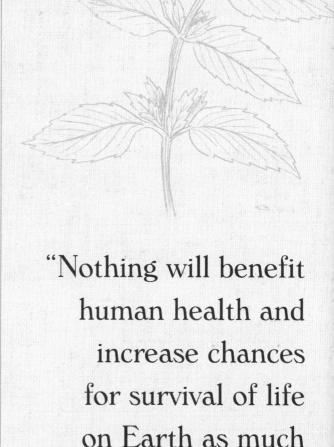

"Nothing will benefit human health and increase chances for survival of life on Earth as much as the evolution to a vegetarian diet."

Albert Einstein

The four pillars

The Farmacy approach to conscious living and healthy eating is based on four philosophical pillars: ancient wisdom, balance, conscious positive intention, and living without harming animals.

1. Ancient wisdom

Thousands of years ago, great philosophers from the lands of ancient Egypt and Greece talked about the idea of food as medicine. One of the earliest books ever discovered was found in ancient Egypt and contained recipes hand-written on scrolls of papyrus. These recipes used herbs, oils, plants, and spices to cure ailments: the first prescriptions in recorded history. They were given up by the Egyptian philosophers as divine offerings to their gods.

Ancient Egyptians placed great importance and emphasis on being healthy and preserving health. Personal names and greetings used in everyday exchanges and letters reflected the culture's emphasis on wellness. Egyptian names were often formed using the word *seneb* which translates as "healthy with vigor and strength." Popular names for ancient Egyptians translate as "I possess health" and "May your father be healthy." Many of the popular greetings of the day were based around the idea of wishing good health to others.

We have adopted some of this ancient wisdom in our philosophy and recipes using plants, herbs, and spices in creative combinations to help maintain health and heal common ailments using food as medicine (*see* pages 18–27).

We also actively support farmers who follow the old principles of organic and biodynamic farming and who grow food in healthy, nutrient-rich soil, without using harmful chemicals and pesticides.

Organic farming combines traditional approaches to growing, supported with the latest farming technology, to benefit the environment and grow nourishing produce free from toxicity.

Biodynamic farms support a holistic approach of farming with the seasons and promote integration of all living organisms within the farm ecosystem—farmers, plants, animals, and insects—all working together in rhythm with the seasons, just as our ancestors did.

2. Balance

To live well and be healthy, we need to find the right balance in all things. We need time to create, work, rest, play, eat well, exercise, get fresh air, spend time with others in our community, enjoy quiet time, support people, have fun, and do all the things that give us a healthy life balance.

The recipes in this book are created with balance in mind. The food is designed to offer balanced nourishment that supports the body and mind, helping to create a healthy approach to nutrition and taking care of yourself.

3. Conscious positive intention

In recent years, there's been great interest in the power of the mind and the strong effects of setting out clear positive intentions. The mind is a mighty tool. This is something the ancients knew well and the secrets of using mind power were whispered and written about through secret societies for generations. Now this information is readily available and is becoming adopted and understood on a mainstream level.

Quantum physics has begun to explain through science what the ancients were saying thousands of years ago that thoughts are powerful and shape our experience in ways that are far stronger than we realize. The strength of our thoughts and intentions is much greater than many of us imagine.

The more we bring conscious awareness to the food we eat and the nature of the quality of that food, the more we build better understanding of our bodies, food habits, choices, and relationships with one another and the planet.

4. Living without harming animals

The Farmacy philosophy is to enjoy a diet that does not cause suffering to animals. From an intuitive point of view, as well as from researching what is happening in the meat industry behind the scenes, we are taking a greater interest in the way we care for all animals.

Not only can practices followed within the meat industry severely impact the well-being of the planet, but the design of the human digestive system seems to suggest that animal protein is not meant for human consumption. Unlike carnivores, which have a short intestinal tract that allows meat to pass quickly through their system, our intestines are longer, like those of other plant-eaters, giving the body time to absorb the nutrients from plant-based foods. Eating meat is therefore linked to poor digestion in humans and means that we are more likely to ingest artificial hormones, chemicals, secondary toxins, and parasites that can be found in meat products. Our bodies are designed to get all the nourishment they need without consuming meat or dairy. There are so many great alternatives available that transitioning to a meat-free diet has never been easier.

"Day by day, what you choose, what you think, and what you do is who you become."

Heraclitus

Good for you

Plant-based eating is wholesome, highly nutritious, ethical, and sustainable. There are a range of health benefits to be gained from this type of eating; studies show that it can help in the prevention of some major illnesses and offers a more compassionate approach to the care of animals and the environment.

A well-rounded diet

An organic, plant-based approach to eating can provide all the nutrients needed for a well-rounded diet. For example, many people who eat a plant-based diet have higher intakes of the potassium-rich foods that help reduce blood pressure, corresponding to a reduction in stress and anxiety, compared with those on other diets. It is possible to consume a broad range of healthy nutrients that fully support health and well-being without eating any meat, dairy products, or refined sugar. There is a lot of data to support these findings.

Increased energy and wellbeing

We have high energy levels when eating natural wholefoods and following a plant-based diet. There are many world-leading sportsmen and women eating plant-based diets and excelling in sports that require physical stamina, energy, and levels of peak performance.

Good gut health

A healthy gut is the fundamental basis of a healthy body, and many diseases begin in the gut. When we eat a varied diet high in fiber, with wholefoods such as grains, seeds, and legumes, we can increase healthy gut bacteria, which in turn helps and supports the health and wellness of the whole body. Studies suggest that diets low in plants and high in animal products can significantly increase inflammation inside the body and disrupt the healthy flora of the gut.

> "Wherever life plants you, bloom with grace."
>
> French proverb

. . . and good for the planet

A plant-based diet is also good for the health of the environment and kinder to animals. Growing plants has a less negative impact on the environment than raising animals for food. With a global shift away from farming livestock for food, we can reduce the impact of deforestation, greenhouse emissions, and the erosion of natural resources. Animals enjoy life, rather than being raised in often terrible conditions before being slaughtered for food.

Cutting greenhouse gas emissions

Currently the food and farming industry accounts for at least ten percent—and possibly as much as 33 percent—of global greenhouse gas emissions. Leading scientists have acknowledged the positive role of organic farming both in tackling climate change and in securing a more sustainable food supply system that can provide food for everyone in the future. Soil stores carbon, and organic soil stores more carbon than nonorganic soil, contributing to the reduction in greenhouse gases needed to address climate change.

Avoiding chemicals and toxins fed to animals

Buying organic food and being mindful about food sources helps cut down on ingesting poisonous chemicals and sprays that are widely used in mainstream food production. Consuming meat and animal products increases our exposure to dietary antibiotics, artificial hormones, industrial toxins, mercury, lead, and other heavy metals. For example, a high proportion of people are now intolerant of cow's milk. Our intolerances to certain food groups are likely to be made worse by the many chemicals and medicines fed to dairy and other livestock and added to the food chain. There are many alternatives to consuming dairy products. At Farmacy we love making our own nondairy milk, butter, and yogurts (*see* pages 74–9).

Food as medicine

Lifestyle and health

One of the exciting things about making healthy food is the alchemy that happens when ingredients are combined in a specific way, creating something that tastes amazing and unlike anything you've tried before.

Food fuels our bodies and provides the catalyst for the chemistry and biological transmissions that happen inside the cells and organs, providing us with the elements we need for energy creation and good health. The better the quality of fuel we give our bodies, the more good health, well-being, and positive emotion we feel.

The intuition that ancient philosophers and traditional well-being systems, such as Chinese medicine and Ayurveda had about the relationship between diet and health is once again coming to the fore as science explores this area. It is now accepted that the modern Western diet, high in processed foods and deficient in fresh wholefoods, is a major contributing factor to current levels of heart disease, cancer, diabetes, and autoimmune diseases. Links are being discovered between diet and brain health, fertility, and mental health.

Now that it is widely accepted that a poor diet has affected human health in a negative way, science is increasingly looking at the positive effects a good diet may have on our health and happiness, from the incredible anti-inflammatory properties of a spice such as turmeric, to the health-giving fermented foods that help replenish the good bacteria in the gut, essential to address many of the digestive issues that affect so many people today.

At the heart of new food science is the message that a plant-based, wholefood diet with little or no processed food is one of the best ways to improve our health. Including foods and cooking techniques that support digestion, and reducing foods that strain digestion, such as meat, sugar, dairy products, and gluten, allows the body to absorb more nutrients and enjoy new levels of energy. This goes back to our theme of simple abundance— cooking and eating foods that have had as little interference as possible from farm to fork.

Food alchemy

The idea of food alchemy has been a core principle in putting together the recipes for this book. We've used alchemy to create the dishes, bringing together unique combinations of real foods, and we've also used only basic cooking techniques, including roasting, boiling, baking, and sautéing. That's it. It doesn't get any more complicated than these four basic cooking techniques. There is no point in making recipes too difficult. We do use a food processor and some basic kitchen gadgets, but essentially the recipe techniques are straightforward and easy.

Digestive health through alchemy of food

The alchemy of eating involves not just your food choices and the combination of foods you eat. It also means working with your body to eat complementary food groups that require the same sort of enzymes to digest the food effectively.

Good digestion

✓ Fresh organic vegetables and fruit are high in water, making them easily digestible.

✓ The fiber in plant-based food helps to move the food through the body, speeding up transit time through the gut, resulting in less fermentation and putrefaction in the intestine. This is good for preventing diseases and improving digestive health. We need plenty of fibrer to stay healthy.

✓ Go for whole grains instead of refined grains. Even if you're not allergic to gluten, gluten-free whole grains such as quinoa, millet, and teff are easier to digest and free from the potential allergens present in some glutinous grains, such as wheat, barley, and rye.

✓ Eat food that helps your body produce healthy bacteria, including coconut yogurt and fermented foods such as kimchi, miso, and sauerkraut, all of which contain plant-based probiotics. These help the body produce good bacteria to keep the gut in best condition.

Bad digestion

✗ Processed food causes stress in the body and slows down digestion, depleting the body of nutrients, and creating a feeling of low energy. The body takes nutrients from other places in the body to aid digestion. Processed food has a negative impact on the immune system, too.

✗ Both red meat and processed food have been linked to digestive cancers, such as liver and colon cancer. Try to avoid both in a healthy, plant-based diet.

✗ Meat is hard to digest and can stay in the digestive tract for long periods because it lacks fiber and water. As a result, animal flesh may become stuck in the intestines as impacted feces that can create toxicity inside the gut.

✗ Parasites are present in raw and undercooked meat and can cause disease and gut-bacteria deficiency. Many unhealthy parasites can enter the body through meat.

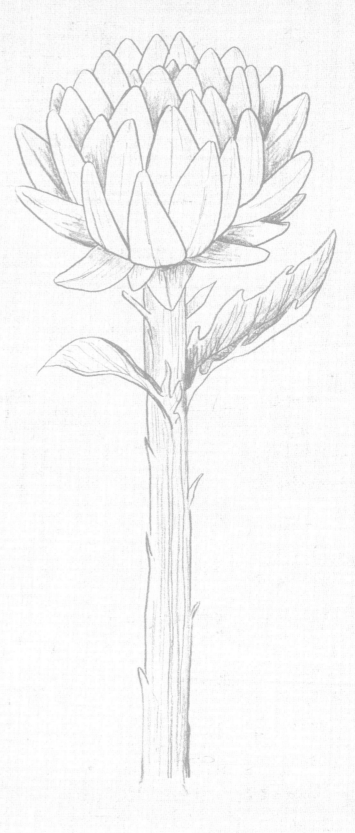

Making good food choices

✓ Be aware of what is being served and whether it contains meat or other animal products. Ask questions about the food you buy and eat.

✓ Get tested for food allergies and make changes to what you eat if necessary. Common allergens include gluten, dairy products, nuts, and corn.

✗ Reduce or eliminate processed foods as far as possible.

✗ Cut down or out caffeine, fizzy drinks, alcohol, deep-fried food, refined sugar, refined grains, canned food, junk food, meat, meat products, nonorganic soy.

✓ Try mono meals from time to time—eating just one type of food at a meal—and see how it makes you feel and how much energy it gives you.

✓ Choose a plant-based diet.

Fruit

The body needs a lot of energy to process unripe fruit.
Fruit is packed with nutrients and contains high levels of fruit
sugar (fructose) so should be eaten in moderation. In other words, don't
assume that eating as much fruit as possible is a good thing. Including fresh,
ripe fruit in your diet is healthy in small amounts.

✓

Eat fruit when ripe.

✓

Sweet and acid fruits are best eaten separately to help you digest them better.

✓

Fruit should make up a maximum of 15 percent of your daily food intake.

✗

Melons are high in sugar. Eat them on their own and not with other foods.

✗

Don't eat fruits and vegetables together. Digesting them requires different
enzymes and the body digests them at different rates. Eating them at the same
time can lead to bloating and gas.

✓

When drinking fruit juice, dilute it with about 80 percent natural,
filtered water to make the juice more digestible.

Fasting

Fasting has a powerful effect, improving all aspects of health—body, mind, and spirit. Cutting out food for a cetain length of time allows the body time to naturally rest, rejuvenate, and recharge itself. Fasting is part of the cultural and spiritual heritage of many countries around the world. It has a powerful and positive effect, regenerating and powering up the body's systems.

There are different approaches to fasting. Some people use liquid nourishment in the form of raw juices and whole juices; others only drink water. Do some research and find what is best for you and your body to give your stomach and digestion a rest and a chance to reset.

One-day fasts can cleanse the body and mind and help restore energy levels and boost feelings of well-being. Stored toxins are released during a fast, the body can feel tired and achy, and emotions can surface to be cleared. This is all part of the cleaning-out process. Take advice on how to fast and how to begin eating again after fasting. It's good to return slowly to eating, consuming a small quantity of light food to begin with to allow the digestion to come back to work gently. Fasting can make a real difference to your health and you will really appreciate the taste of good food again afterward. If you have any medical concerns, always take advice from a healthcare professional.

Research the right approach for you and test a few different methods to find the one that best suits you and your body.

Forgiveness
Acceptance
Self-control
Truth
Integrity
Nourishment
Grace

"I fast for greater physical and mental efficiency."

Plato

Dairy detox

Dairy products are regularly genetically modified, unless certified organic. Factory-farmed cows are injected with antibiotics and growth hormones that enter the milk supply. Cows are often fed genetically modified grains grown using toxic pesticides and these easily transfer into milk and meat products. Humans are the only species who regularly and systematically drink another animal's milk.

Many dairy cows are kept in inhumane conditions that have an impact on the animal's health, and the stress and fear they experience is likely to have an effect on the milk they produce. Drinking milk from mistreated cows that have been artificially inseminated to keep them lactating has an inevitable impact on human health and well-being. Many people are intolerant or allergic to dairy foods. We advocate moving away from dairy products and enjoying plant-based alternatives instead.

People often ask how they can consume sufficient calcium without eating dairy products. The dairy industry advertising campaigns of the past did a good job in establishing the belief that milk is essential for calcium and instilled the incorrect idea that milk is the only way to get enough in our daily intake. Calcium exists in many plants and seeds and it's straightforward to get the right daily levels of calcium from eating plant-based food.

In fact, eating animal products leaches calcium from the body, but calcium can be found extensively through the plant kingdom in dark green leafy vegetables including spinach, kale, broccoli, watercress, mustard greens, and seaweed. These foods all supply calcium to the body. Many legumes, nuts, and seeds are also a good source of calcium, including lentils, chickpeas, white beans, and black beans. Sesame seeds, for example, are rich in the mineral and are great for adding to salads and dishes. They form the base of the tahini that we use in many Farmacy recipes (*see* page 68). There are many easy ways to obtain calcium from eating plants.

> "The time will come when men such as I will look upon the murder of animals as they now look upon the murder of men."
>
> Leonardo da Vinci

The Alchemy of Conscious Living

The more attention we pay to the way we live,
the food we eat, the conversations we have,
the choices we make, what we buy, and how
we treat the Earth's resources, the more
chance we have of making better and more
empowering decisions that will lead to
a healthier, more sustainable future for
everyone. How we spend our time, who
we spend time with, the ideas we think
about, our actions, and the words we
speak all have a powerful impact
on health and well-being.

Conscious eating

Conscious eating not only raises your awareness about what you are eating and putting into your body but also why, when, and how you eat. In the rush of modern life, we have lost some of our natural connection with food and don't always take the time to notice what we are going to eat.

In conscious eating, you pause, taking the time to appreciate the food you are about to eat. You take a good look at it, smell it, and feel some joy at the prospect of what you are about to eat, and then take your time to taste it consciously. This is an important part of digestion and helps us to power up the quality of good digestion. If you eat while watching your cellphone or catching up on messages, an important part of the natural digestion process gets missed.

Eating mindfully helps digestion and generates feelings of appreciation. When we eat with awareness, the food tastes better somehow; it feels as though we are nourished in a deeper way, and our bodies digest the food more completely. The first phase of digestion, called the cephalic phase, works best when the body is relaxed and when we pay attention to the process of eating.

Digestion and nourishment are improved when we become conscious of the process through smelling, seeing, tasting, chewing, and swallowing. Through these instinctive processes, the body sends signals to the gut and digestive tract with detailed information that causes the release of the specific enzymes needed to break down the food that is on its way. The more consciously we eat, the better our digestion becomes.

Stress interrupts and slows down digestion significantly. If you suffer from poor digestion, bring awareness back by eating more slowly and consciously. It will make a big difference to your body's ability to assimilate food and nourish itself.

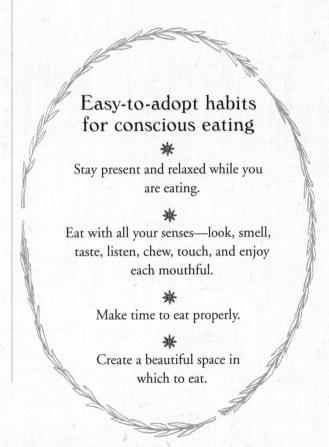

Easy-to-adopt habits for conscious eating

✳

Stay present and relaxed while you are eating.

✳

Eat with all your senses—look, smell, taste, listen, chew, touch, and enjoy each mouthful.

✳

Make time to eat properly.

✳

Create a beautiful space in which to eat.

Digestion starts with a thought

Pavlov, with his dogs, was the first person to show in a scientific study that animals start salivating at the thought of a meal. In other words, they have a physiological digestive response due to thoughts alone. Since then, we have discovered that many physical digestive responses happen in the first stages of digestion, before any food reaches the stomach. These include salivation, secreting stomach acid, and activating digestive enzymes to digest proteins, carbohydrates, and fats.

Our experience of appetite is almost like a dance between the brain and the stomach, one signaling to the other to make us feel either hungry or satiated. Studies have shown that when eating mindfully, with awareness, physical feelings of satiation occur earlier than when eating without care and attention.

Stress and good digestion are opposites

The part of the nervous system that works in conjunction with digestion is the "rest and digest" part of the system. A stress response causes the body to go into "fight or flight," the opposite of the mode for digesting, taking the blood flow away from our digestive organs to the extremities, so we can flee if necessary.

Feeling stressed means we don't produce the enzymes we need to tackle the processing of food. The bottom line is that when we get stressed, digestion is significantly compromised. The best way to help your body absorb nutrients and digest food is to avoid stress, to focus on eating when you do eat, and to avoid multitasking or eating on the run. Take your time and give eating the space it deserves. It's important to stay away from too many distractions, upsetting conversations, computer screens, and anything that pushes our stress buttons, in order to be calm and relaxed enough to digest food fully and completely.

"Imagination is everything. It is the preview of life's coming attractions."

Albert Einstein

Using all the senses

Using all our senses, and being aware of how they work together, is one of the secrets to optimal digestion. When we were testing recipes for this book, we had friends over to test and give feedback on the dishes we were creating. For one part of the trials, we asked the tasters to eat mindfully in silence and words of thanks were given before everyone started eating. There was a much greater appreciation of the food when eating silently and this was a profound effect but not surprising. Everyone said that they noticed more about the food. They noticed the color, texture, and feel of the dish and felt a sense of love for what they were eating. Every person reported that they appreciated the food offered far more than when they were engaged in discussions, and that they felt much more gratitude for the food and one another.

Smell

Smell is a guide to effective digestion; it tells us if food is fresh or has turned rancid. It creates a connection and an association with the emotional center of the brain.

When we smell aromas we love, strong emotions are triggered and natural chemicals are released into the body. When our sense of smell is altered and we cannot smell easily, for example, if we have a blocked nose from a cold, then our appetite and ability to taste food is affected. Good smell creates good digestion and makes the food so much more enjoyable. Our smell receptor, the nose, is located directly over the mouth in the perfect position to smell and approve the food we are about to eat.

Taste

When we are deciding what to eat, we tend to choose by focussing on a mixture of the five main taste indicators—salty, sweet, sour, bitter, and umami. In fact, we use all the senses in the complex process of choosing, eating, and digesting food. Chewing food helps develop the taste and appreciation of flavors that, in turn, sends information to the body to get it ready for action and digestion.

Umami is one of the five basic tastes, along with sweetness, sourness, bitterness, and saltiness. It comes from a Japanese word meaning "a pleasant, savory taste." We detect umami through taste receptors that recognize an amino acid called glutamate. This amino acid is found in many savory foods, such as seaweed broths, shiitake mushrooms, green tea, foods fermented with bacterial or yeast cultures, and nutritional yeast.

Scientists consider umami to be a distinct taste on its own because we use specific receptors in our mouth to recognize this quality instead of using a combination of other taste receptors to do so. Fermented sauces based on umami taste were used widely in ancient Roman as well as medieval cuisine and as early as the third century in China.

Umami was first discussed in 1908 by Kikunae Ikeda, a professor at Tokyo Imperial University. He noticed that the taste of *kombu dashi* (vegetarian stock used in Japanese cooking) was different to the tastes sweet, sour, bitter, and salty. He named this new taste "umami" and it's now used today to describe a fifth taste.

In the 1950s, scientists discovered that a greater and more intense umami flavor was created when foods that were rich in glutamate were combined with other foods containing ribonucleotides, such as shiitake mushrooms. When these foods are combined, they produce a deeper intensity of taste than each of the ingredients produces individually.

In our recipes, we use the alchemical principle of creating deeper and more intense flavors by combining certain ingredients.

Sight

The recipes in this book are colorful and designed to look beautiful. When we look at food, it triggers important physiological processes. The more colorful and fresher food looks, the more we want to eat it and the more we feel excited by it. The sensory receptors in our eyes do a great deal of work in triggering digestion. We can see whether food looks as if it is starting to rot, and choose to steer clear if something doesn't look right or appetizing.

The way we see food and the amount of food on a plate is affected by the size and shape of the dishes it's served on. There's a phenomenon called the Delboeuf illusion. Studies have shown that bigger plates make a serving of food appear smaller, which results in people misjudging how much they eat. The sight of the food in relation to the size of the plate makes a difference in perception, so choose portion size and presentation carefully.

Harmonizing with the environment includes spending time making your food setting beautiful. At Farmacy we like to keep it simple and might set the tables with some fresh flowers, a pretty tablecloth, or something from the garden representing the food and the season. Make beautiful crockery important in your arrangement. If everything works together it adds to the enjoyment of the food in a wonderful way.

Sound and touch

Chewing is important and listening to the crunch of textures gives the body important information that is decoded by the digestive messaging system. So, chew and then chew some more. It's easy not to chew food enough. We're often so busy rushing around that chewing well is often something we forget to do properly.

For digestion to work at its best, it's good to slow down the process and begin to be consciously aware of chewing. The more time we spend consciously chewing, the better the food is broken down by enzymes in the mouth. Chewing also allows enough time for the gut enzymes to do the job of assimilating the food's nutrients.

Conscious choices

An increasingly large percentage of everything we buy is discarded and goes to waste within six months of purchase, and most waste is not biodegradable. Bringing greater awareness to how we manage our garbage is essential for a healthier and sustainable world.

We create billions of tons of waste every year and the quantity is rising. All the garbage and the way we manage the mountain of trash we produce every year is a big issue.

Say no to plastic

More food and products are covered in plastic than ever before, and this is causing big problems for the health of planet Earth. Plastic litters cities, the countryside, the oceans, and waterways and contributes to health problems for all living creatures, not just humans. Plastic pollution is a serious threat to the environment because plastic creates toxic exposure in every phase of its life cycle. Every year, millions of single-use cups and billions of plastic bottles are thrown away worldwide, and these numbers are rising fast.

Plastic does not fully degenerate. It breaks down into smaller pieces and is eaten by marine life, or it degrades into a form of plastic dust. Millions of marine animals and seabirds die every year as a result of eating or becoming tangled in plastic. Nearly every piece of plastic ever made and thrown away still exists, because there is no process or organism that can break it down fully.

When we store food in plastic wrapping or containers, chemicals can leach into food and create toxicity. In the restaurant, we avoid using plastic and choose biodegradable materials for our packaging and straws. We also employ eco-friendly solutions for cleaning, soaps, and general kitchen use.

How to reduce your plastic footprint

Say no to plastic bags; use reusable bags made from eco-friendly material such as hemp.

Buy fresh food from markets and local farm suppliers. Say no to nonbiodegradable packaging.

Do not buy plastic bottles. Get a water filter to improve water quality at home and carry a reusable water canister.

Say no to plastic straws when they are offered in restaurants and bars.

Choose products packed in boxes rather than plastic bottles.

Buy biodegradable garbage bags and product packaging as far as possible.

Store food in glass containers, rather than plastic, to prevent chemicals from leaching into food.

Look for the new wave of retailers that encourage customers to bring reusable containers from home to fill up with staple ingredients.

Chemical-free farming

In the past, farming was carried out without using toxic pesticides and harmful chemicals. All food was organically grown, that is, grown without chemical additives. Starting in 1945, farmers began to add chemicals to the soil and sprayed them on plants to kill insects and creatures that ate the food crops during the growing season.

It has taken us decades to realize that chemicals that kill insects may not be good for humans either. We are now seeing the negative health effects of allowing these chemicals to become more established and part of the food chain over the last 60 years. Chemicals used in growing crops enter the food through its skin and through the direct absorption of water in the soil. We are contaminating food from the inside out, so while washing the skin of vegetables and fruit helps it doesn't rid the food of all the chemicals that the food absorbs into its cells through the soil and skin membrane.

Much of the food grown by conventional methods is sprayed extensively, and many times, during the growing season to make it look good, keep insects away, and to prevent blemishes on the skin, helping farmers sell it more easily. At Farmacy our food is organic wherever possible, and we buy food in its whole, raw form, sourcing regional and local produce. We prefer to make everything in the house from scratch to make sure that it is high quality and free from chemical additives.

Pesticides uncovered

The pesticide industry is worth billions globally, and the big chemical companies that make pesticides and fertilizers have a great deal of power and involvement in many research studies. Some studies are partly funded by the biggest pesticide companies in the world, and these have excluded some very important effects on health for "cost reasons." If these negative health effects had been included in the studies, the outcomes would have been very different, and likely to have compromised the reputation of the chemical corporations.

When we see images of people wearing gas masks and all-in-one protective overalls to keep them safe while spraying our crops, we need to start asking more questions about industry standards and the health problems caused by the widespread practice of coating the food and land with chemicals.

"If food is medicine, how we produce food is key. Farmacy is supporting agro-ecology and regenerative agricultural practices that remineralize the soil as well as helping support bio-diverse soil, to help us survive and thrive in a well nourished society with a flourishing biosphere. It is in creating a diverse microbiome in the soil that we begin to cultivate a civil society. We are truly civilized when we are well nourished."

Emma Goodwin, biodynamic farmer

Soil quality

The nutrient quality of soil has become depleted and out of balance as a result of applying chemicals, while soil nutrient levels worldwide are reaching seriously low levels that are causing international concern. Agricultural industries around the world must pay closer attention to how to resolve the situation and make this a priority. Growing uncontaminated food in nutrient-dense soil is one of the most significant and pressing needs facing the world today.

Organic standards

Organic certification requirements vary in different countries. The general principles usually specify at least that:

• Land should not have been treated with toxic chemicals and fertilizers for three years prior to organic certification.
• Details of the methods and materials used in growing are recorded and monitored.
• No genetic engineering, irradiation, or sewage sludge is allowed.
• Soil fertility and crop nutrients must be managed through specific cultivation practices.

Sustainability

Organic agriculture supports environmentally and economically sustainable food production and works closely with nature. Organic farming focusses on crop rotation and using animal manures, plant compost, and bio-based pest control. When buying from organic growers, we know that food has been produced using fewer chemicals on the land. The water from farming goes directly into the waterways. Organic farming encourages wildlife and biodiversity.

Asking questions

When actively engaging in conscious living, it's important to know where food is grown. Does it meet organic standards (including no pesticides) and is the quality of the soil it was grown in sustainable?

Natural beauty at home

At the end of this book we've included some natural beauty and home recipes to help you start making your own skincare range using ingredients with no added nasties or chemicals. Making all-natural cosmetics, skincare, and house-cleaning products not only saves money, but also gives you the confidence of knowing that they are organic. Added to this you will have the pleasure of making them yourself with love in your own kitchen.

"Farmacy is the first place I have really enjoyed eating the food. As a biodynamic grower, I'm lucky to be eating fresh and tasty vegetables all year round and I'm usually disappointed by food when I eat out. There is so much thought and care around how to prepare food here so that it not only tastes good but also makes the body feel wonderful. I love the creativity and beauty of this food."

Dorothea Leber, biodynamic farmer

In the Farmacy Kitchen

We share a handy at-a-glance list of ingredients and store cupboard essentials. This section has all the information you need for preparing nuts, seeds, beans, and grains as well as a simple guide on how to grow your own sprouts. After the easy preparation, it's quick to put together the recipes that follow with the nourishing and activated ingredients.

Store cupboard essentials

Remember to choose organic products and to buy the best quality food possible. We like to use independent suppliers to support local businesses and organic food sources. Search out your nearest farmer's markets and health food stores. You will find that many of the ingredients here are now stocked either in supermarkets or health food stores. You can always build up your store cupboard over time as you try the recipes and become used to some of the less familiar ingredients.

Kitchen staples

Bee pollen
Buckwheat groats
Cacao
Chia seeds
Chickpeas
Coconut, desiccated
Coconut, cold-pressed oil/butter
Coconut nectar
Coconut cream
Dates
Dijon mustard
Flaxseeds, whole (mill at home
   for best nutrients)
Goji berries
Hemp seeds
Honey (raw)
Maple syrup
Millet
Miso, brown rice (organic,
   GMO-free, gluten-free)
Mushrooms, dried, particularly
   shiitake

Mustard, organic Dijon
Nutritional yeast
Nuts: almonds, cashews,
   hazelnuts, macadamias,
   pecans, pistachios, walnuts
Oats (gluten-free)
Probiotic powder
Quinoa
Seeds: hemp, pumpkin, sesame,
   sunflower
Sea vegetables: dulse, kombu,
   nori, wakame
Tahini
Tamari (organic GMO-free)
Teff flakes

Herbs and spices

Asafetida (optional: can be
   used when cooking beans)
Black pepper
Cayenne pepper or chile flakes
Cinnamon
Cloves
Coriander seeds
Cumin
Fennel seeds
Ginger
Nutmeg
Salt: sea salt, Himalayan pink salt
   and salt flakes (avoid regular
   table salt because it is often
   industrially produced and can
   contain unhealthy chemicals)
Turmeric

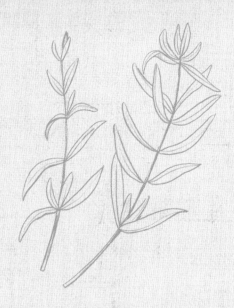

Flour
Buckwheat
Gram
Rice
Tapioca
Teff

Oils
Coconut, cold-pressed, virgin
Olive, cold-pressed extra-virgin
Sesame: regular and toasted
Sunflower

Vinegars
Apple cider
Rice
Sherry

Home and beauty
Activated charcoal
Bentonite clay
Peppermint oil (food grade)

Egg replacement

We use chia or flaxseeds to
replace eggs in recipes. As a guide,
use 1 tablespoon of flaxseeds or chia
seeds mixed with 2½ tablespoons of
water to create a plant-based "egg."
Soak the seeds for 15 minutes and
you have a great replacement.

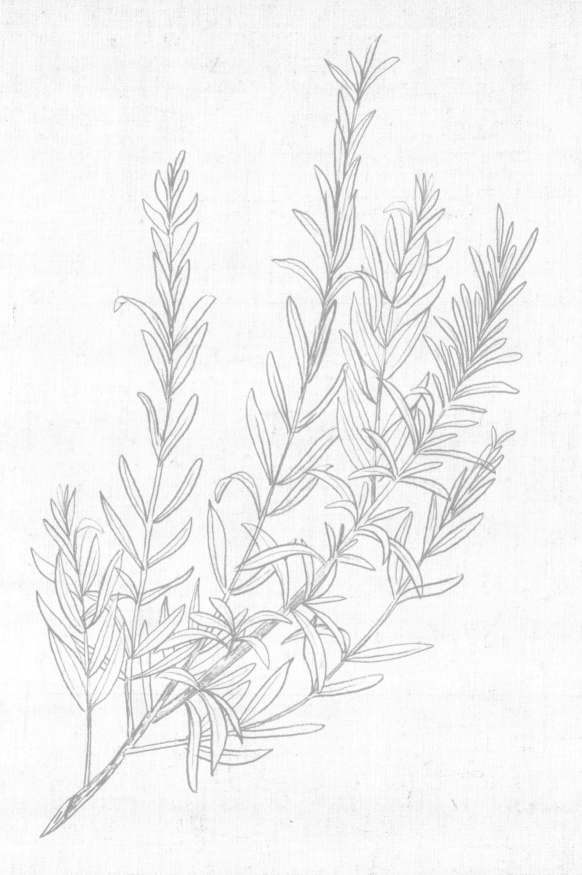

Sprouted
mung beans

Fruit chia jam

Fermented
kimchi

Sprouted
beans

Cashew
yogurt

Vegetable broth

Seaweed
broth

Tahini sauce

Nut milk

Green sauce

Nut butter

Seaweed

Rice

Dates

Philosopher's sauce

Alchemist's sauce

Cranberry beans

Farmacy seed mix

Fermenting kimchi

Salt

Lima beans

Walnuts

Sprouting mung beans

Olive oil

Kitchen equipment

A high-quality food processor
This is a good investment for a plant-based kitchen. Choose one with a range of attachments and a large bowl. An additional smaller bowl is useful for blending dips, dressings, and sauces. They are expensive but will last a long time. Most good brands come with a guarantee of several years.

Blender
A high-speed blender does a different job to a food processor. Use it to blend juices, smoothies, soups, or nut milks and to process nut flours.

Electric citrus juicer
This small gadget makes extracting citrus juice easy. It is fast, easy to use, and simple to clean. Cut the citrus fruit in half, push one half on top of the juicer, and it filters out the pulp and seeds in seconds. The juice is delivered into a glass below the spout.

Electric hand-held mixer
A simple hand-held electric mixer is a handy addition and used in some of the recipes.

Sprouting jars
Buy a selection of sprouting jars for home sprouting. These jars have a mesh lid made from cheesecloth or loosely-woven fabric, which allows air to reach the sprouts and makes them easy to drain.

Salad spinner
A good old-fashioned salad spinner is a useful tool to clean and dry salads and sprouts. We wouldn't be without one in the Farmacy kitchen.

Nut milk bag
Choose a sustainable and compostable version made from hemp and cotton rather than a synthetic nut bag. These bags have a multitude of uses, as well as separating the pulp in nut milks. They can also be used as a bag to hold herbs and spices when making soups and stews, for nut cheeses, as a colander for soft ingredients, or as a giant teabag to hold your favorite loose-leaf tea in a glass jar or teapot. Keep it handy, give it a rinse after use, or put it in the dishwasher to clean it ready for the next job. We use nut milk bags every day.

Cutting boards
Choose wooden boards over plastic. Wash, rinse, dry, and wipe with the cut side of half a fresh lemon to keep it fresh and sanitized.

Good knives
Investing in a set of knives with sharp blades will save you time, enable you to chop finely, and make food preparation a breeze. Ceramic blades work well. Keep your knives in good condition with regular sharpening to help with precision cutting, which makes the food look good.

Mandoline slicer
A useful gadget to evenly slice food into varying widths and thicknesses. Create slices, waffle cuts, crinkle cuts, or dice firm vegetables and fruits. Choose one that is easy to clean and safe to use. Read the reviews because there are different types and styles to choose from.

Pressure cooker

Pressure cookers are designed to retain more of the nutrients in the food and to reduce cooking times by up to half (and we all like to save time in the kitchen). For example, cooking beans in a pressure cooker reduces the cooking time from 2 hours to 20 minutes. The quality of pressure cookers has improved significantly in recent years and they're much easier to use than in the past. They are not essential, but help save time and energy.

Strainers

Have fine and medium-gauge strainers in your kitchen and choose strainers made from a non-plastic and eco-friendly material.

Flasks and water bottles

Keep a selection of food-grade vacuum-insulated stainless steel flasks and reusable water bottles at home. They keep drinks fresh and you will never need to buy water in a plastic bottle when you are out. Check that there are no plastic liners in the flask that might leach chemicals into your drinks.

Storage containers

Glass or food-grade stainless steel containers are best for storing, freezing, and carrying food. Traditional plastic containers can transfer chemicals—such as Bisphenol (BPA)—into food. We recommend avoiding plastic containers for storage, staying BPA-free (look at labels when buying), and choosing glass or food-grade metal storage. Avoid using aluminum foil for cooking and wrapping food. Wrapping food in foil and then heating it, especially if it is acidic and spicy food at a high temperature, can cause leaching of aluminum into the food. Head for nonplastic and nonaluminum alternatives and use paper bags to store food, and parchment paper or waxed for baking and wrapping food.

Water filter system

The quality of tap water varies significantly depending on where you live. Tap water can contain fluoride, chlorine, pesticides, and heavy metals in varying amounts. It's worth checking the quality of your water (there are inexpensive kits available to help you do this) and consider water filters or tap filter systems to improve it.

Cookware

Reducing your exposure to toxins and staying free from chemicals means paying attention to the pans you use in the kitchen. Take a close look at the quality and materials of your cooking pans. Look for eco-friendly and "green" ware when choosing a healthy range of pans.

Ceramic cookware is a healthy choice. Ceramic enameled cast-iron cookware is popular and versatile. These pots can go from stove to oven and have a good nonstick surface. When cleaning, be careful not to chip or scratch the surface. Clay crock pots are great for roasting. They retain heat after cooking and keep food warm on the way to the table. Always check if the glazes used on the pots contain toxins, such as lead. Read the label and research the quality of your cooking pots carefully before buying.

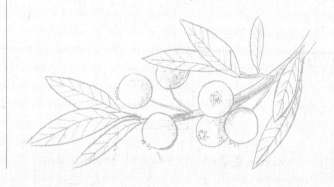

Some people believe that stainless steel saucepans are safe and others claim that if you use them to cook acidic food, they can leach nickel, cobalt, and chromium into the food. Nickel is present in stainless steel and can cause allergies. To test if it's present, take a magnet and check how magnetic the pan is. The more magnetic it is, the less nickel is present.

Glassware is safe and nontoxic to use. Glass is not as good a conductor of heat as ceramic, but it is toxin free and safe to use for cooking.

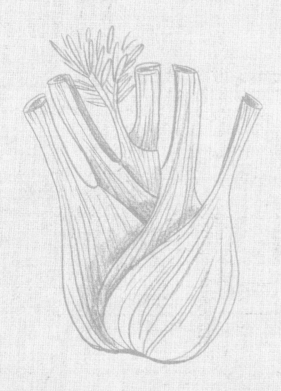

Avoid aluminum. It is not a safe material for cooking with because it has been linked to Alzheimer's and dementia. When heated, aluminum leaches into food easily, especially when cooking acidic foods. Because it heats up quickly, some pans have an aluminum core inside a safer metal one. The problem is that if the surface is damaged, food can be exposed to aluminum. It's best to avoid cooking food in any pan that contains traces of this metal. Copper pans are also best avoided as studies show that copper can leach out and using them for cooking may mean consuming more than the recommended daily dose, which can be harmful.

Teflon became popular because it prevents foods from sticking. It's easy to scratch and, if damaged, the surface layer of Teflon can get into the food and be ingested along with it. Scratched Teflon can expose the surface underneath, which is often a harmful metal, such as aluminum. Teflon releases toxic fumes when heated and it's not advisable to breathe these in or absorb them into the body

Plastic should not be used when cooking. When heated or microwaved, the toxic chemicals it contains go straight into food and have negative effects on health. Many plastics leach xenoestrogens or BPA when heated. These are artificial hormones that cause hormonal imbalances. This is why you should never heat a plastic container or put hot food or liquid into plastic bowls. Reheating fast food in plastic containers or ready meals bought in a plastic tray may leach chemicals and toxins into the food and this is not a healthy method of heating.

Preparing nuts, seeds, grains, and beans

Nuts, seeds, grains, and beans offer some of the best sources of essential nutrients, including vitamins, dietary fiber, healthy fats, and proteins. We use them regularly in the Farmacy kitchen to create nutrient-rich dishes, crunchy textures, and creamy sauces.

Activating nuts and seeds by soaking makes them a much more potent source of vitamins and nutrients. When raw nuts and seeds come into contact with water, they come alive and shoots begin to grow. Many varieties have enzyme inhibitors to protect them from damage in their early stages of growth. These inhibitors slow down the natural absorption of nutrients and are neutralized by the soaking stage, making the nuts and seeds more nutritious and easier to digest. Traces of dust or tannins are washed away during soaking, making them taste better, too.

As a general guide, denser nuts need longer soaking. But do be careful not to soak them for longer than the recommended time (*see* chart below) because this can compromise the flavor, texture, and nutritional benefits.

Soaking is best done at room temperature. For most nuts, the easiest way to do this is to soak them overnight and rinse and drain them in the morning.

The nuts and seeds we love to use give a great range of flavors and they are highly versatile. Cashews add a creamy, mild taste to dishes; almonds are bursting with nutrients and have a health-boosting alkalizing quality; while walnuts are known as "brain food" thanks to their high levels of omega-3 fatty acids.

Soaking nuts

Almonds	overnight	Raw almonds contain more nutrients than any other nut, including vitamin E, calcium, phosphorus, iron, and magnesium. They also contain zinc, selenium, copper, and niacin and can be ground into flour.
Cashews	1 to 2 hours	These have no enzyme inhibitors, so need less soaking. They contain monounsaturated fats, iron, and minerals, including copper, magnesium, thiamine, calcim, and niacin. They are high in starch, making them good for dips, creams, and as a thickening agent.
Pecans	4 to 6 hours	Contain more than 19 vitamins and minerals, including vitamins A and E, calcium, magnesium, potassium, and zinc. Just 1oz (¼ cup) provides about 10 percent of daily recommended fibre intake.
Walnuts	1 to 2 hours	Have a high concentration of omega-3 fatty acids and antioxidants.

Walnuts

Cranberry beans

Quinoa

Sunflower seeds

Soaking seeds and grains

Buckwheat	Flaxseed	Millet	Quinoa	Rice	Sunflower	Teff
8 to 12 hours	8 hours	8 to 12 hours	8 to 12 hours	8 to 12 hours	4 hours	8 to 12 hours

The cooking time of grains is shorter if they have been soaked. Soaking also makes the grains more easily digestible and nutritious.

To soak the grains, add 2 tablespoons of lemon juice or a flavorless vinegar (or use less depending on how much you like an acidic taste) to 6½oz of your grain of choice and add warm water to cover.

Put the grains, juice or vinegar, and water into a saucepan and let stand overnight.

The longer the grains soak, the less water is needed and the shorter the cooking time required. Reduce the water specified on the package by 25 percent and also the cooking time by 20 percent if you have soaked the grains.

After soaking, rinse the grains thoroughly until the water runs clear. They are then ready to cook.

Cooking seeds and grains

	Buckwheat	Millet	Quinoa	Basmati rice	Brown rice	White rice
Water (oz and cups)	4fl oz (½ cup)	12fl oz (1½ cups)	12fl oz (1½ cups)	10½fl oz (1¼ cups)	18fl oz (2¼ cups)	8fl oz (1 cup)
Cooking time (minutes)	5	10 to 15	10 to 15	20	35	15
Resting time (minutes)	20	20	20	20	20	20

The cooking times in the chart above are for 6 ounces of dry grains. Be sure to add ¼ tablespoon salt to the water before cooking.

The grains will need some time to fully absorb the liquid once you remove the saucepan from the heat. Let stand, covered, for 20 minutes.

You will have perfectly cooked grains if you allow them this time to absorb all the liquid.

Dry roast the soaked millet before cooking by stirring it in a pan over medium heat until it smells toasted, to obtain loose grains that don't clump together.

Activating nuts and seeds

Rinse the nuts or seeds, put them in a large glass bowl or jar, and add water. Cover with a lid or light cloth and soak for the time specified on the soaking chart (*see* pages 49 and 51). Then rinse again and store in the fridge for one or two days.

Dehydrating nuts

Preheat the oven to its lowest setting, spread the nuts out on a baking pan, and bake them for several hours. Alternatively, put them in a dehydrator for 24 hours, until they are crisp. When nuts have been activated and dehydrated, they can be kept in a sealed container in a dry and dark place for several months. If the nuts are not completely dried out first, they can get moldy, so it is important to make sure that they are absolutely dry before storing.

Making nut flour

It's easy to make nut flour at home. Good nuts for making flour are almonds, cashews, and hazelnuts. Make sure the nuts are fresh and use blanched almonds for flour or it will become almond meal.

Put the nuts into a blender, grinder, or food processor and whizz them for 8 to 10 seconds until the mixture has the texture of flour. Make sure not to overblend and stop blending before the nuts become too much like butter in consistency.

Store in a dry, sealed container in a dry, dark place.

A note on nut allergies

✳

Some people experience serious allergic reactions to nuts. It's important to check for nut allergies when preparing food for a group and ask about any possibility of nut intolerance.

Sprouting

Sprouts are 10 to 30 times more nutritious than vegetables. They are one of the most nutritious of all wholefoods and full of flavor. By ingesting sprouts as living food, you take the energy from the shoots directly into your body. At the sprouting stage, plants have the strongest concentration of nutrients in their life cycle. Sprouts are easily digestible because of their delicate cell walls.

There are many advantages to home sprouting. For example, they are easy and cost effective to grow. As the sprout grower, you know they are chemical-free. It doesn't take long to start sprouting at home and you will have access to living food packed with nutrients all year round. When you add water to the seeds, they begin to sprout small shoots as they move into the growing phase. During the first few days of sprouting these little shoots are at their most potent and nutritionally dense stage, bursting with enzymes, vitamins, and minerals.

How to sprout

Take a large preserving jar with a metal lid that can hold a cheesecloth cover, or use a glass jar and cover it with a clean cloth. Place the seeds in the bottom of the jar and put the cover on. Pour three times more water than you have seeds through the cloth, swirl the seeds, drain, and discard the water. Cover again with fresh water. Soak overnight.

Next day, rinse the seeds in water, swirl, and drain again. Continue to rinse, swirl, and drain over the next few days until small white sprouts appear. During hot weather, you may need to rinse and drain the seeds two or three times a day. The sprouts will continue to grow until they have filled the jar.

Dry the sprouts as thoroughly as possible (use a salad spinner if you have one). If they are stored wet, they will quickly rot. Keep them in the fridge, ideally in an airtight container. Make a note of the date and mark an end date for using them on the jar to make sure you eat them fresh. They will last 7 to 10 days when stored correctly.

These steps only take a couple of minutes a day, and will give you plenty of living, delicious, and nutritious sprouts ready to eat. Sprout heaven!

Soaking and sprouting times

	Soaking time	Sprouting time
Alfalfa	5 hours	5 days
Broccoli	8 hours	4 days
Chickpea	12 hours	3 days
Fenugreek	6 hours	5 days
Lentil	8 hours	3 days
Mung bean	8 hours	3 to 5 days
Quinoa	6 hours	1 to 2 days
Radish	6 hours	5 days
Sunflower	6 hours	24 to 48 hours

Mung beans, soaking

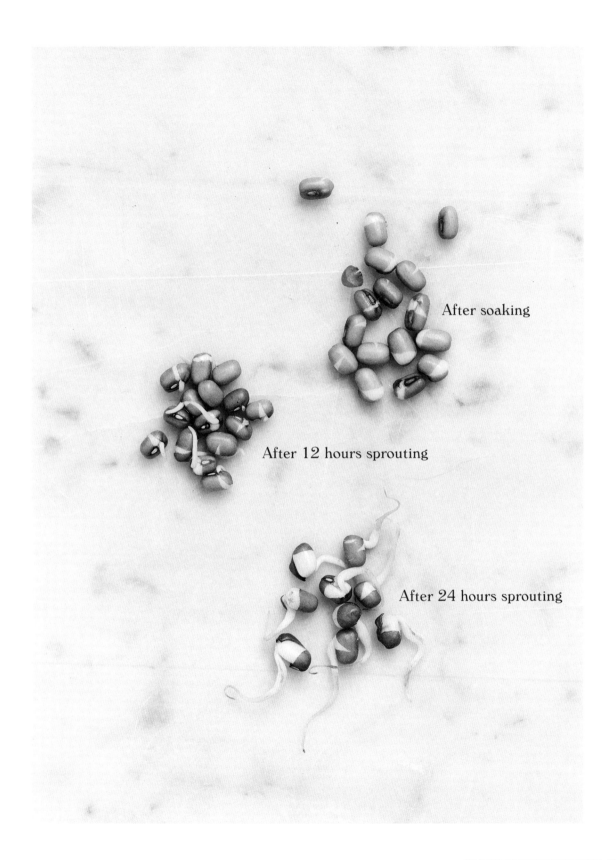

After soaking

After 12 hours sprouting

After 24 hours sprouting

Cooking with beans and pulses

We love using beans, pulses, and legumes in our recipes. Steer clear of the canned varieties to avoid preservatives and soak and cook your own. This guide tells you all you need to know about handling beans and pulses as well as giving you some of our best bean hacks.

Different beans have different soaking and cooking times (*see* chart right). It takes a few hours to cook beans in a regular saucepan. You may like to use a pressure cooker to reduce cooking times.

Choose organic and buy in bulk where you can from retailers supporting a no-waste policy that allows you to take your own refillable container. Check that the beans are fresh and do not look wrinkly. When they are more than 12 months old, beans begin to lose their fresh taste. If you aren't sure about the age of beans, ask the retailer to place a special order.

Soaking beans is important. It reduces the cooking time and helps the body digest them more easily. You may need to build up the enzymes required to help your body digest beans well. Start by eating small legumes (lentils, azuki) and when you can digest these easily, move up to a medium-size bean such as black or pinto beans. Then move on to bigger ones, such as red kidney beans and chickpeas.

Eating a lot of beans and pulses can result in extra air and gas in the body. This is because beans contain a sugar called oligosaccharide. Humans lack the enzyme required to break down this sugar, so when it arrives in the lower intestinal tract, it can ferment and cause a build-up of gas. The gas isn't absorbed into the intestine, and the body has to expel it, creating that not-so-lovely windy effect.

To stop the gas when eating beans, start by laying out the dry beans and sorting them for quality, discarding any stones and dried out or discolored beans. Put the beans in a container, cover with water, and let stand to allow the beans' sugar to be released. Change the soaking water a few times to prevent the beans from reabsorbing the sugar.

Place the beans in a pan of fresh, clean water, adding ½ onion, ½ tablespoon of salt, and a dried bay leaf. To help break down the sugar further in order to avoid the gas effect add two pinches of either asafetida or baking soda, or a 4-inch piece of kombu (a type of kelp) and bring to a boil. Skim off any foam that rises to the surface during cooking. When they are completely soft the beans are fully cooked. Most beans require a second cooking to create some of the dishes in the recipes.

The exception to this is lentils, which should only be cooked once and can become mushy if cooked for too long. Cook lentils according to the guidelines on the right, adding chopped carrots and celery to give more depth of flavor. Add peppercorns and Farmacy Seed Mix (*see* page 80) and an equal volume of liquid to lentils.

Aquafaba

Aquafaba is the common name for the cooking liquid from beans and legumes, and it is usually thrown out after the cooking process. It contains a unique mix of starches, proteins, and other soluble plant solids that have dissolved during cooking. Aquafaba is very versatile, and has a wide range of uses, including emulsifying, foaming, binding, and thickening. It can be used to replace egg whites in many recipes too, such as in our Alioli (*see* page 114).

Bean soaking and cooking times

Type of dried bean, 7oz	Soaking time	Regular cooking time	Pressure cooking time
Black	4 to 6 hours	45 to 60 minutes	15 to 20 minutes
Chickpeas	Overnight	1½ to 2½ hours	15 to 20 minutes
Lentils	1 to 2 hours	20 to 30 minutes	Not recommended
Mung	Overnight	15 minutes	Not recommended
Split mung	30 minutes	8 to 10 minutes	Not recommended
White	Overnight	45 to 60 minutes	4 to 5 minutes

Tips

Soaking and cooking times vary for different
kinds of bean. If you're using more than one
kind of bean in one dish, cook them separately.

You can use the cooled cooking water (only if
unsalted) to water the houseplants. They love
bean water.

Be sure to boil and skim the froth from
the beans before cooking them om a slow cooker
or pressure cooker.

In this section, you'll find a range of basic recipes that we use regularly at home. We suggest you start by making these and keep them on hand in the kitchen. Many of them store well and they will all give you a great starter kit for the dishes that follow. With these basics prepared, you're good to go.

Basics

Vegetable Broth

This golden broth is full of goodness and forms the basis of many dishes in our kitchen. In it, vegetables and spices come together to create a deep flavor and provide good nutrition. This broth is an elixir that packs a big hit of vitamins and minerals with a slightly spicy kick. It's also delicious as a broth on its own and you can add your favorite spices to enjoy on a cold winter's day.

Quantity: 1 quart
Preparation time: 20 minutes

1 celery stalk, cut into 4

2 onions, quartered

1 carrot, quartered

1 turnip, quartered

1 fennel bulb, including the fronds, quartered

2 tablespoons olive oil

1 head of garlic, halved horizontally

1 slice of fresh ginger root, about ½ inch thick

3 cloves

1 bay leaf

6 black peppercorns

1 bunch of parsley stems

1½ quarts water

1½ tablespoons salt

Put all the ingredients into a saucepan over medium heat and bring to a boil. Reduce the heat and simmer gently for 15 minutes, then turn off the heat. Strain off the liquid and use as necessary.

This broth can be stored in an airtight container and kept chilled for 3 to 4 days, or frozen.

Seaweed Broth

Farmacy Seaweed Broth is inspired by an ancient Japanese recipe. It's a highly nutritious, mineral-rich base that is a great way to add depth of flavor without using fats or additional salts. We use it in a range of recipes, including Philosopher's Sauce and many soups. It's also used to soak chia seeds to give extra flavor to the Farmacy Caesar Salad (*see* page 156).

Quantity: 1¼ quarts

Preparation time: 30 minutes, plus 1 hour soaking

2 pieces of dried kombu, each about 6 inches long, soaked overnight in 1¼ quarts water

4 dried shiitake mushrooms

½ tablespoon salt

Put the soaked kombu and its soaking water into a saucepan over medium heat and slowly bring to a boil. Just before the water boils remove the kombu (it's important not to boil kombu or it will become bitter). Keep the kombu, as it can be reused one more time before needing to be discarded.

When the water boils, reduce the heat to low and add the shiitakes. Cook for 1 minute, skimming the surface, then turn off the heat. Let the saucepan stand for an hour, then strain the broth.

Store for up to a week in a sealed jar in the refrigerator, or freeze.

Philosopher's Sauce

Philosopher's Sauce is Farmacy's take on classic Asian fish sauce. It's a great way to add a deep umami taste to dishes such as Thai curries and noodles. This is a highly nutritious base which we use in a range of Farmacy recipes and has all the goodness of Seaweed Broth and black garlic combined.

Quantity: 1 cup
Preparation time: 15 minutes

2 cups Seaweed Broth (*see* page 61)
1 black garlic clove, crushed
2 garlic cloves, crushed
1¼ tablespoons salt
¼ cup tamari
1 teaspoon sherry vinegar

Place all the ingredients in a saucepan and bring to a boil. Lower the heat to a simmer and reduce the liquid to half the amount. This will take about 15 minutes.

Store in a dark, dry cupboard for up to three months. This sauce doesn't need to be refrigerated.

Green Sauce

Our magic Green Sauce is a raw sauce inspired by "schug'" or "zhug," a hot chile sauce of Yemeni origin. It packs a punch of flavor whenever it is added to a dish. We use Green Sauce for a flavor lift in salads and other dishes, such as Eggplant Rolls (*see* page 120). It mixes well with Tahini Sauce (*see* page 168) as the flavors complement each other. Chiles contain fiber and a range of vitamins and minerals, including iron, magnesium, potassium, copper, and manganese. The cilantro and lemon aid digestion and help support the immune system.

Quantity: 1 cup
Preparation time: 5 minutes

2 garlic cloves
1 to 2 green or jalapeño chiles
1 teaspoon Farmacy Seed Mix (*see* page 80)
1 large bunch of cilantro, stems and leaves
½ cup sunflower or canola oil
2 tablespoons lemon juice
½ teaspoon salt

Put the garlic, chiles, and seed mix in a food processor and blend together. Add the cilantro, oil, lemon juice, and salt. Process until the sauce is smooth, like pesto. Check the seasoning and adjust if necessary with more lemon juice.

Keep in an airtight container in the refrigerator for up to 1 month. The color may darken over time due to oxidation, but this doesn't affect the flavor. You can top with a thin layer of oil to prevent oxidation, or alternatively, freeze half to use another time.

Tahini Sauce

GF NF R VG

Use this versatile, oil-free sauce any way you like. It is one of our favorites in the Farmacy kitchen range and combines well with Green Sauce (*see* page 66) for a flavor made in heaven. It's rich in protein and minerals, including magnesium, potassium, and iron. We use it as a creamy, nutritional hit in many of our dishes and love loading it onto salads or adding it as a topping to fresh vegetables.

Quantity: 2½ cups
Preparation time: 5 minutes

1 cup tahini
½ cup lemon juice
½ teaspoon salt
¾ cup water

Mix the tahini, lemon juice, and salt in a blender and gradually add the water to create the desired consistency.

Store sealed in a jar with a screw-top lid in the refrigerator for up to a week.

Alchemist's Sauce

GF NF R VG

This is one of the main sauces we use to add depth of flavor. It tastes similar to Worcestershire sauce and is full of natural goodness. We use Alchemist's Sauce in our Caesar Salad dressing (*see* page 156) and as a special ingredient in the raw zucchini dressing of the Farmacy Macro Bowl (*see* page 164). This wonderful sauce adds a new level to the umami of plant-based food preparation. It tastes great in a Bloody Mary, too!

Quantity: about 1¼ cups
Preparation time: 5 minutes

1 cup apple cider vinegar
¼ cup tamari
1 tablespoon coconut nectar
½ date, soaked for 30 minutes
¼ teaspoon ground ginger
1 coin-sized piece of fresh ginger root
¼ teaspoon Dijon mustard
1 tablespoon thinly sliced onion
1 garlic clove, crushed
¼ teaspoon ground cinnamon
¼ teaspoon black pepper
¼ teaspoon coriander seeds
¼ teaspoon fennel seeds
½ teaspoon tamarind sauce

Place all the ingredients in a jar, screw the lid on securely, and shake vigorously. Shake it again. Let stand for 30 minutes to allow the flavors to develop, but no longer or the garlic will begin to overpower the other ingredients. Strain the liquid into a glass bottle and seal with a lid.

Keeps for up to 3 months. This sauce does not need to be refrigerated.

Fruit Chia Jam

GF NF R VG (if using maple syrup)

This is a healthy chia jam to spread on toast, add to desserts, or to top a probiotic yogurt breakfast. It has no refined sugar and a fresh and fruity flavor. Chia seeds are full of fiber, proteins, omega-3 fatty acids, and many other nutritional goodies. They are great for the digestion, too.

Quantity: about 4½oz

**Preparation time: 5 minutes, plus
  30 minutes chilling**

1 cup mixed fresh fruit, peeled, cubed,
  or pitted as necessary (we used mango,
  blackberry, and raspberry)

2 teaspoons honey or maple syrup

2 teaspoons lemon juice

2 teaspoons chia seeds

Place the fruit in a blender with the honey or maple syrup and the lemon juice. Blend until it reaches a soft and jammy consistency.

Stir in the chia seeds. Put in the refrigerator for 30 minutes to allow the chia seeds to expand.

Store in an airtight container in the refrigerator for up to 7 days.

Almond Butter

This recipe is a one-ingredient wonder that transforms almonds into a luxurious, velvety spread. We use it as a butter replacement in our recipes and in a variety of plant-based dishes. Almonds are high in vitamin E and are one of the most nutritional of all nuts. The butter adds flavor and thickens sauces with all the nutty goodness that almonds provide.

Quantity: approximately 9oz
Preparation time: 20 minutes, plus
** 15 minutes cooking**

1lb 2oz raw, skinned almonds, unsoaked

Preheat the oven to 300°F. Place the almonds on a baking pan and put in the oven for 15 minutes. Be careful not to color the nuts too much; do not fully toast them.

Place the nuts in a food processor and process at high speed for 2 minutes. Reduce to medium speed and process until the mixture has a creamy texture similar to tahini, and is smooth and velvety. If there are still lumps, continue processing.

The mixture will go through different states, turning from almond meal to powder and then into butter. Be patient and scrape the bowl frequently, especially at the start. The time it takes will vary depending on the freshness of the nuts, and can take up to as long as 15 minutes.

Notes

This is one recipe for which you don't need to soak the almonds. The almond butter works best when the nuts' natural oils are warmed, allowing them to be released more easily.

This recipe does not work with ready-ground almonds. Raw, skinned almonds produce a creamy and velvety butter texture free from the solids of the skin. Alternatively, you can use almonds with their skins to create a darker butter with a slightly different flavor.

This keeps well in an airtight container in a dry, cool place.

Cashew Yogurt

GF R VG (if using maple syrup)

This probiotic-rich yogurt can be eaten alone, used to make sauces, or added to dishes as a creamy, good-looking garnish. This makes a large jar of delicious yogurt that helps keep the gut healthy, maintaining gut flora and enhancing general wellness.

Quantity: 3 cups

Preparation time: 10 minutes, plus 2 hours soaking, plus 24 to 36 hours fermenting

1½ cups unsalted raw cashews, soaked

1¼ cups water

¼ teaspoon probiotic powder or 2 probiotic capsules

¼ teaspoon vanilla powder (optional)

1 tablespoon honey or maple syrup (optional)

pinch of salt (optional)

Drain and rinse the cashews, then place them in a blender with the water and probiotic powder or capsules. Blend until smooth with a consistency similar to custard.

Place the yogurt in a clean, lidded jam jar and cover with a clean dish cloth or a piece of cheesecloth. Leave some space at the top of the jar for the yogurt to develop without overflowing the container.

Keep in a warm place (try the top of the refrigerator) for 24 to 36 hours. The longer you leave the jar undisturbed, the tangier the yogurt will be. It's ready when the mixture appears foamy and comes away from the sides of the jar. It should have a strong and pleasant, tangy aroma.

When the yogurt has fermented, return it to the blender and blend again, adding the optional ingredients, if using.

Transfer to a glass container with a lid, cover, and store in the refrigerator for up to a week.

Nut & Seed Milk

GF NF (if made with seeds)
R VG

Drinking nut milk is a healthy way to have milk without eating dairy products. Nut milks are versatile and can be used on cereals, in drinks, to add creaminess to smoothies, and as a healthy base for sauces and purées. This is a highly nutritious milk full of protein and goodness. If you get into the habit of soaking nuts every night, you can whizz up some fresh nut milk the next morning.

Quantity: 1 quart

Preparation time: 10 minutes, plus soaking time

5½oz nuts or seeds, soaked
(*see* soaking chart, pages 49 and 51)

1 quart water

½ teaspoon vanilla powder (optional)

1 tablespoon coconut oil (optional)

2 tablespoons sweetener or 3 pitted dates (optional)

pinch of salt (optional)

Rinse and drain the soaked nuts or seeds thoroughly. Put in a blender with the water, blend, then strain through a nut milk bag or cheesecloth into a bowl.

Clean the blender. Return the milk to the blender with the optional ingredients, if using.

This keeps for 3 to 5 days sealed in an airtight container in the refrigerator.

Note

Cashews have no skin so they don't need to be strained.

Farmacy Seed Mix

This seed mix takes food way beyond classic seasoning. It deepens flavors, taking dishes to a whole new level. This mix appears in many of the recipes in this book. Make a batch and keep it in the kitchen to use as needed. This recipe was inspired by chef Peter Gordon. We use it frequently in the Farmacy kitchen.

Quantity: ⅓ cup
Preparation time: 5 to 10 minutes

2 tablespoons each cumin, coriander seeds, and fennel seeds

Put the seeds in a dry skillet without oil over medium heat and cook them until they are fragrant. This takes about 3 minutes. The aim here is not to toast the seeds, but to release the beautiful combination of flavors by warming the seeds together in the pan.

Put the seeds in a food processor and pulse and blend until they have a consistency you like.

Store in an airtight container in a dry, dark place for up to 6 months.

Here's a range of great ways to begin the day in Farmacy style. There's porridge, a smoothie bowl, seed bread, and a feast of other good, nourishing breakfast dishes to kick-start your day in a healthy way.

Breakfast

Soothing Porridge

GF NF (if pistachios not used)
VG (if honey not used)

Millet is one of the best-kept health-food secrets. It's high in nutritional value and has been eaten by many ancient cultures for centuries. The flavor is deliciously nutty and surprisingly creamy when cooked. It's also gluten-free. This version of porridge is a great alternative to the more common seeds and grains. It is a good source of protein, calcium, iron, zinc, magnesium, and essential fats, helping to support heart health, protecting from diabetes, improving digestion, and detoxifying. With the addition of ginger, turmeric, vanilla, and cinnamon, it's also anti-inflammatory and full of antioxidants.

Serves 2
Preparation time: 20 minutes, plus 8 hours soaking

½ cup millet, soaked for 8 hours, or overnight
1 teaspoon coconut oil
¼ teaspoon ground cinnamon
¼ teaspoon ground ginger
¼ teaspoon ground turmeric
¼ teaspoon vanilla powder
1 cup coconut milk, plus extra if needed
1 cup water
pinch of salt

Toppings
2 to 4 small figs, quartered
2 tablespoons honey (optional)
handful of chopped pistachios (optional)
1 teaspoon hemp seeds

Rinse the millet in a fine-mesh strainer under running water and then drain.

Preheat the oven to 350°F. Place the figs in an ovenproof dish and bake for 15 minutes until they are juicy and syrupy.

Heat the coconut oil in a small saucepan over medium heat. Add the cinnamon, ginger, turmeric, and vanilla and stir. When fragrant, after about 30 seconds, add the rinsed millet and a pinch of salt and stir to coat for 2 to 3 minutes, lightly toasting the millet.

Add the milk and water and stir. Bring to a boil, then reduce the heat, cover, and let simmer gently, stirring often to make sure it doesn't stick to the bottom of the pan. After about 15 minutes most of the liquid should have been absorbed and the porridge will have a thick and creamy consistency. If the mixture looks dry before the grains are tender, add a little more coconut milk.

Spoon into bowls and top each with figs, honey (if using), pistachios (if using), and hemp seeds.

Probiotic Jar

GF R VG (if honey and bee pollen not used)

This recipe will give you a beautiful probiotic parfait jar. We serve it at the restaurant and people always say how lovely this jar looks. Probiotic yogurt is full of good bacteria, which stabilize the gut, and the addition of spirulina makes it rich in minerals and protein. Chia is great for speeding up digestion, as well as being high in omega-3s. Enjoy taking care of your gut health with this beautiful jar of goodness.

Makes 4 x 9fl oz servings
Preparation time: 25 minutes

For the chia pudding

2 cups homemade Nut & Seed Milk (*see* page 78)

1 tablespoon honey or other sweetener (optional)

½ teaspoon vanilla extract

⅓ cup chia seeds

For the probiotic spirulina yogurt

2 cups Cashew Yogurt (*see* page 76)

¼ teaspoon vanilla powder

1 tablespoon raw honey or other sweetener (optional)

½ teaspoon spirulina powder

pinch of salt

To serve

1 cup strawberries, sliced

2 tablespoons bee pollen (optional)

¼ cup coconut chips

¼ cup sliced almonds

To make the chia pudding, blend the nut or seed milk with the honey (if using) and vanilla extract in a mixing bowl. Stir in the chia seeds until well combined. Soak until the seeds have absorbed all the liquid and become gelatinous. This mixture will keep for 3 days in a sealed container in the refrigerator.

To make the yogurt blend all the ingredients together in a high-speed blender until well combined.

To assemble, put a layer of strawberry slices around the edge of the bottom of a parfait jar and add some yogurt. Spoon a layer of chia pudding on top of this. Finish with more strawberry slices, the bee pollen (if using), coconut chips, and sliced almonds.

Protein Omelet

Serves 4
Preparation time: 25 minutes, plus
5 minutes cooking

For the omelet
1½ cups water
2 cups chickpea flour
⅓ cup olive oil
¼ teaspoon salt
¼ cup coconut oil, for frying, divided

For the creamy harissa sauce
1¼oz carrots
1 red chile
1 tablespoon Farmacy Seed Mix
1 garlic clove, crushed
1 tablespoon olive oil
¼ cup chopped onion
6oz red bell pepper, chopped
¼ cup chopped tomato
pinch of paprika

For the yogurt cream
⅔ cup Cashew Yogurt (*see* page 76)
2 tablespoons nutritional yeast
salt and pepper

For the filling
2 tablespoons olive oil
2 garlic cloves, finely chopped
14oz chard or stemmed spinach, leaves and
    stems separated

To serve
Roasted Red Pepper Confit (*see* page 208)
sprouts
cilantro

A recipe inspired by socca *Niçoise* from the South of France. This delicate chickpea flour omelet is a fresh and healthy alternative to the traditional egg kind and can be served with a combination of fillings. We add chard, a yogurt cream, and a roasted carrot harissa sauce. Chickpeas and cashews are a great source of protein and provide a healthy start to your day.

Preheat the oven to 400°F.

Prepare the omelets by adding all the ingredients to a blender and blitzing until combined. Transfer to a bowl and set aside to rest for 15 minutes.

Meanwhile make the sauce. Place all the ingredients on a baking pan and roast in the oven for 25 minutes. Remove and allow to cool slightly before adding to a food processor. Blend until you have a smooth, creamy sauce.

While the vegetables for the sauce are roasting, make the yogurt cream by mixing all the ingredients in a bowl. Set aside.

To make the omelets, heat a small nonstick skillet over medium heat and add 1 tablespoon of coconut oil. Pour in enough batter to create a thin omelet about 6 inches in diameter. Cook on one side until lightly browned and crisp, then flip it over and repeat with the other side. Place on a tray lined with parchment paper and repeat the process, putting a sheet of paper between each omelet as you stack them up. These can be kept in a low oven while you make the filling.

For the filling, heat the olive oil in a large skillet. Add the chard or spinach stems and sauté until softened, about 5 minutes, then add the leaves and continue until just wilted. Add the garlic and toss everything together for a further minute.

To serve, smear yogurt cream on an omelet, top with sautéed chard, a dollop of the sauce, Roasted Red Pepper Confit, a few sprouts, and some cilantro leaves.

Green Smoothie Bowl

GF NF R (if granola not used)
VG (if bee pollen not used)

This fresh, green, and vibrant bowl will wake you up and help you start the day feeling energized and well fueled. It's a great way to consume a healthy hit of vitamins and minerals in the morning. The ingredients blend well together, allowing for optimum digestion and nutrition at the start of your day.

Serves 2 to 3
Preparation time: 10 minutes

3 peaches, pitted
½ banana
½ avocado
4½oz fresh spinach
1¼ cups coconut water
10 mint leaves

To serve
Sprouted Quinoa Granola (*see* page 94)
   (optional)
bee pollen (optional)
fresh berries
mint leaves

Put all the ingredients in a blender and whizz until smooth and colorful.

Pour into bowls and decorate with granola (if using), bee pollen (if using), fresh berries, and mint leaves.

Sprouted Quinoa Granola

This recipe offers you a delicious nut-free and grain-free seed granola bursting with nutrients and vitamins.

Serves 12

Preparation time: 10 minutes, plus soaking and sprouting, plus 40 minutes cooking

1 cup Homemade Apple Sauce (*see* opposite)

¼ cup maple syrup

3 tablespoons tahini

1 teaspoon vanilla extract

12oz sprouted quinoa (*see* page 53)

½ cup sunflower seeds

½ cup pumpkin seeds

2 teaspoons ground cinnamon

pinch of salt

¼ cup raisins

¼ cup goji berries

Preheat the oven to 300°F. In a small bowl mix together the Apple Sauce, maple syrup, tahini, and vanilla until you have a thick paste.

In a large mixing bowl, combine the quinoa, sunflower and pumpkin seeds, cinnamon, and salt. Pour the apple sauce mixture over the quinoa and seeds and stir to combine.

Spread the granola evenly over a baking pan lined with nonstick parchment paper and bake in the oven for 20 minutes. Remove the pan, stir the granola minimally to ensure you keep nice big clumps, and bake for another 20 minutes, until toasted.

Allow the granola to cool, then stir in the raisins and goji berries. Store in an airtight container.

Homemade Apple Sauce

A healthy breakfast accompaniment for a tangy contrast of flavor, providing a good source of fiber, vitamin C, and loaded with plenty of beneficial anti-oxidants.

Quantity: 1 quart
**Preparation time: 10 minutes,
  plus 20 minutes cooking**

10 medium apples (most varieties
  will work but a sweet variety will
  eliminate the need to add sweetener),
  peeled, cored, and sliced
1 cup water
pinch of ground cinnamon (optional)
sweetener of choice (optional)
squeeze of lemon juice (optional)

Put the apple slices in a large saucepan, add the water, and cover. Bring to a boil over medium-high heat, then reduce the heat and simmer, stirring occasionally, until the apples break down into a thick sauce. This will take about 20 minutes.

Pour the cooked apple into a blender and whizz until smooth. Taste and add any of the optional ingredients to taste.

Store in a refrigerator for 1 week, or freeze.

Fluffy Pancakes

GF NF (if nut milk not used)
VG

Everyone loves pancakes and this recipe offers a healthy, gluten-free version of the family favorite. The buckwheat is a nourishing and energizing alternative to the flour traditionally used to make pancakes. Buckwheat is nonallergenic and contains high levels of rutin, which helps combat high blood pressure, and there are plenty of easily digestible proteins here, too. This is delicious as a breakfast dish or a dessert.

Serves 5
Preparation time: 25 minutes

½ cup gluten-free oat flour (or whizz rolled oats in a blender to make flour)

¾ cup buckwheat flour

1 cup unsweetened Homemade Apple Sauce (*see* page 95)

½ cup dairy-free milk

2 tablespoons maple syrup

1 teaspoon baking powder

1 teaspoon baking soda

2 teaspoons lemon juice

1 teaspoon vanilla extract

To serve
sliced bananas
fresh berries
Chia Jam (*see* page 72)
coconut yogurt
maple syrup

Place all the ingredients in a blender and purée until smooth.

Heat a nonstick skillet over medium-high heat and, when hot, pour ⅔ cup of pancake batter into the center of the pan. Spread it into a circle with the back of a spoon, keeping it reasonably thick. Cook for 2 to 3 minutes.

Slide a spatula underneath the pancake, flip it over, and cook for another 2 to 3 minutes before removing it from the pan. Put the pancake on a warm plate and cover with a dish cloth. Repeat until you have used up all the batter.

Serve with banana slices, berries, jam, coconut yogurt, and a drizzle of maple syrup.

Seed Loaf with Farmacy Butter

This seedy loaf is highly nutritious and simple to make. We came up with this recipe when we wanted to make tasty bread that helps you feel energized after eating it. The loaf is flour-free and high in protein, as well as containing vitamins, minerals, and good oils. It tastes great toasted and served with butter and Fruit Chia Jam (*see* page 72).

Serves 10 (makes 1 loaf; 10 slices)
Preparation time: 10 minutes, plus 6 hours refrigeration and 1 hour baking

For the loaf
½ cup teff flakes
½ cup gluten-free rolled oats
1 cup ground almonds
2 tablespoons chia seeds
1 cup sunflower seeds
½ cup flaxseeds
3 tablespoons psyllium husks
¼ cup coconut oil
1½ cups water
1 tablespoon apple cider vinegar
1½ tablespoons coconut nectar or other sweetener
1 teaspoon salt

For the butter
½ cup coconut oil
2 tablespoons flaxseed oil
large pinch ground turmeric
pinch of salt

Line an 8-inch loaf pan with nonstick parchment paper.

Mix all the dry loaf ingredients in a bowl. Add the wet ingredients and mix until well combined. Put the dough in the prepared pan.

Refrigerate for 6 hours, or overnight.

When you're ready to bake the loaf, preheat the oven to 300°F. Bake the loaf for 1 hour, until brown. Push a narrow knife into the loaf; if it comes out dry, the loaf is baked.

Make the butter by mixing or blending all the ingredients. Place the mixture in the refrigerator to set.

Serve slices of the loaf toasted and topped with the butter.

Breakfast Loaf

This banana breakfast loaf has a sweetness and texture that is great for the morning, and is delicious topped with some Cashew Yogurt (*see* page 76). Or you could try eating it as a healthy treat in the afternoon with a cup of tea. Blueberries contain one of the highest antioxidant levels of any berry. They help combat aging, boost focus and memory, and promote good skin condition. Bananas provide potassium, fiber, and a range of vitamins. It's important to use ripe bananas for this recipe to give the loaf sweetness.

Serves 10 (makes 1 loaf; 10 slices)
Preparation time: 15 minutes,
   plus 50 minutes baking

3 ripe bananas, plus 1 for the top (optional)

¼ cup coconut oil, melted

⅓ cup maple syrup

1 tablespoon ground flaxseeds mixed with 2½ tablespoons water, and left to stand for 5 minutes

1½ teaspoons vanilla extract

1½ cups gluten-free oat flour (or whizz rolled oats in a blender make flour)

¾ cup ground almonds

1 teaspoon ground cinnamon

1 teaspoon gluten-free baking powder

½ teaspoon baking soda

pinch of salt

½ cup walnuts, chopped, plus extra for decoration

⅓ cup blueberries

Preheat the oven to 350°F. Line an 8-inch loaf pan with nonstick parchment paper.

In a food processor, mix together the bananas, coconut oil, maple syrup, flaxseed mixture, and vanilla extract until well combined. Add the oat flour, ground almonds, cinnamon, baking powder, baking soda, and salt and continue mixing until all are incorporated.

Fold in the chopped walnuts and blueberries, then pour the batter evenly into the prepared pan.

If using a fourth banana, slice it in half lengthwise, and press it into the top of the loaf, cut-side up, and sprinkle chopped walnuts around it. Lightly press the walnuts into the top.

Bake in the oven for 50 to 60 minutes or until a toothpick pushed into the loaf comes out clean. Allow the bread to cool on a wire rack before removing from the pan, slicing, and serving.

We love dips and snacks at Farmacy. This is our collection of favorites to share with you. There are ideas for food on the run, dips to share with friends over drinks, and delicious appetizers to serve before the main event.

Dips & Appetizers

Miso with Hemp Seeds

This dip uses a healthy brown miso without the harmful **GMO** found in some other miso recipes. Enjoy the deep umami flavors of miso with healthy ingredients that support a strong immune system, healthy nervous system, and bone health. The alkalizing nature of the ingredients keeps the body strong and helps to repel infections. Hemp seeds are added for crunch, a magical flavor, and a further boost of good nutrients. This is a great, easy snack to serve any time. Try it with some freshly cut vegetable sticks.

Serves 8
Preparation time: 10 minutes

2 tablespoons lemon juice
2 tablespoons lime juice
2 garlic cloves, crushed
3 tablespoons brown rice miso
2 tablespoons tahini
1 teaspoon sesame oil
½ cup Seaweed Broth (*see* page 61)
1 teaspoon coconut nectar

To serve
cucumber sticks
carrot sticks
hemp seeds

Infuse the lemon and lime juice with the garlic for 10 minutes and then strain and discard the garlic.

Place the infused lemon and lime juice, miso, tahini, sesame oil, broth, and coconut nectar in a food processor and whizz until it has a soft consistency similar to mayonnaise. Refrigerate overnight to allow the flavors to develop.

Just before serving, toast the hemp seeds in a dry skillet. Mix them into the dip and serve with crudités.

Store in an airtight container in the refrigerator for up to 2 weeks.

Mayan Dip with Lime

The inspiration for this dip is an ancient Mayan recipe. It is updated here with a twist, including sun-dried tomatoes and arugula for a fresh, lively taste and a big flavor. The Mayans ate a lot of pumpkin seeds, which provide essential levels of magnesium, zinc, and omega-3 fatty acids. This seed dip is loaded with goodness and essential elements.

Serves 6
Preparation time: 15 minutes

1 cup pumpkin seeds
¼ cup olive oil, divided
1 onion, finely chopped
1 garlic clove, minced
3½oz arugula, chopped
1 green chile, whole
½ cup chopped cilantro
zest of 1 lime
2 tablespoons lime juice
1 tablespoon extra-virgin olive oil
½ tomato, cored and seeded
½ cup sun-dried tomatoes
¼ cup Vegetable Broth (*see* page 60)
salt

Toast the pumpkin seeds in 1 tablespoon of the olive oil. Sprinkle with salt and set aside.

In a skillet gently sauté the onion, garlic, and chile in the remaining olive oil until the onion is translucent. Transfer to a food processor along with the rest of the ingredients. Process for about 4 minutes or longer for a smoother texture.

Tip into a serving bowl and serve.

Store in an airtight container in the refrigerator for up to 3 days.

Pictured overleaf, from left to right:
Mayan Dip with Lime, Farmacy Hummus,
Miso with Hemp Seeds, Spicy Queso

Spicy Queso

The Farmacy kitchen takes on the iconic nacho cheese dip in this fun dish full of healthy ingredients. The eggplant is a great source of dietary fiber, vitamins, and minerals, including manganese, copper, iron, and potassium. The dish is rich in antioxidants and supports cardiovascular health as well as protecting you from free radicals. It tastes pretty good, too! This is a dish to share with friends alongside a bowl of crunchy nachos. It's also easy to make a nut-free version. Just omit the cashews and you're good to go.

Serves 8

Preparation time: 5 minutes, plus 1 hour salting and 30 minutes cooking and cooling

1 medium eggplant, cut into ½-inch slices and salted for 1 hour

1½ cups almond milk (or other dairy-free milk)

1 garlic clove

¼ cup cashews

2 red chiles

1 teaspoon Farmacy Seed Mix (*see* page 80)

¼ cup nutritional yeast

½ medium tomato, seeded and chopped

2 teaspoons tapioca flour

¼ cup olive oil

1 teaspoon smoked paprika

2 tablespoons apple cider vinegar

Preheat the oven to 425°F. Wipe the salted eggplant slices with paper towels, place on a nonstick baking pan, and bake until just turning brown. This usually takes about 20 minutes.

Place the slices in a blender with all the other ingredients and blend until smooth and a thick creamy texture.

This can be stored in the refrigerator for up to 1 week.

Farmacy Hummus

Hummus is a firm favorite in our kitchen. There are many good recipes, but we love this one because it's so velvety, luxurious, and tasty and is packed full of nutrients. This recipe is inspired by the exceptional version of hummus created at the Zahav Israeli restaurant and we think it delivers on flavor and nourishment. The garlic is infused during the process and then removed, instead of being left in. As a result, the hummus has a softer flavor and lasts longer. Mixed with its own cooking broth, the hummus retains all the nutrients from the chickpeas. The addition of spirulina gives it an extra burst of nutrient-rich greens and color. Make plenty; it will be eaten fast!

This recipe uses the chickpea broth before it is thickened and turned into aquafaba (*see* page 56). It's best to use dried chickpeas here. However, if you only have canned chickpeas, mix the aquafaba with an equal quantity of Vegetable Broth (*see* page 60) and use in place of the chickpea water in this recipe.

Serves 6
Preparation time: 5 minutes

4 garlic cloves, unpeeled
⅓ cup lemon juice, plus extra to taste
1 teaspoon spirulina (optional)
1 teaspoon salt
⅓ cup tahini
2 cups cooked chickpeas (*see* page 57),
   ½ cup cooking water reserved
½ teaspoon Farmacy Seed Mix (*see* page 80)
pinch of ground cumin (optional)
paprika and extra virgin olive oil, to serve

Put the garlic, lemon juice, spirulina (if using), and salt in a food processor, whizz, and then let stand for 10 minutes so the garlic mellows.

Strain the mixture through a fine-mesh sieve into a small bowl, pressing on the solids to release as much liquid as possible. Discard the solids.

Return the liquid to the food processor, add the tahini, and pulse to combine. With the motor running, add the chickpea water a little at a time until the mixture is very smooth.

Add the cooked chickpeas and seed mix and process until smooth. Adjust the seasoning with salt, lemon juice, and cumin, if using.

To serve, spoon the hummus into a shallow bowl, dust with paprika, and drizzle generously with extra virgin olive oil.

Store in an airtight container in the refrigerator for up to 4 days.

Goji Ketchup

This is a distinctive and colorful ketchup that you can use whenever you want a healthy sauce with a burst of flavor to add to your food. Goji berries contain a high dose of antioxidants and are a good source of protein and vitamin C. This delicious condiment has a load of nutrients that support healthy skin, too. A perfect accompaniment for our Baked Chickpea Sticks (*see* page 198).

Quantity: 8
**Preparation time: 5 minutes,
    plus 20 minutes soaking**

½ cup dried goji berries
¼ cup sun-dried tomatoes, halved
14oz can whole peeled tomatoes
3 teaspoons apple cider vinegar
2 tablespoons maple syrup
2 teaspoons lemon juice
¼ teaspoon onion powder
1 teaspoon olive oil
½ teaspoon salt
pinch of pepper

Soak the goji berries and sun-dried tomatoes in a bowl of water for 20 minutes. Strain and discard the soaking water. Drain the canned tomatoes and discard the liquid.

Blend all the ingredients together in a food processor. Taste and add further seasoning to taste.

Keep in an airtight container in the refrigerator for up to 1 month.

Alioli

This is our no-egg version of alioli. The liquid from cooking chickpeas, called aquafaba (*see* page 56), replaces eggs and adds nutrients. When we give this lush and creamy dip to friends, they can't tell the difference between this and regular alioli, which we take as a great compliment.

We always think it's best to use aquafaba from cooking fresh, dried chickpeas. However, we make an exception here and recommend using the liquid from canned chickpeas as it emulsifies better.

Serves 4
Preparation time: 5 minutes

2 tablespoons aquafaba (*see* page 56)
1 tablespoon Dijon mustard
1 garlic clove
1 cup safflower or sunflower oil
2 tablespoons lemon juice
salt

Place the aquafaba, mustard, and garlic in a food processor and process at medium-high speed for 10 seconds.

Clean the sides of the food processor and set at medium speed, using the setting for mayonnaise if your machine has one.

Slowly add the oil in the thinnest possible stream; this will take about 4 minutes. It is important to add the oil very slowly because the aquafaba needs time to emulsify. Then add the lemon juice and salt to taste and serve.

Store in an airtight container in the refrigerator for 3 to 4 days.

Satay Sauce

A healthy and easy version of a classic Thai-inspired satay sauce. This is a quick and nourishing way to dress up roasted vegetables. You can also serve it with chickpea sticks, add it to a stir-fry, or use it as a delicious topping on noodles. Peanuts are a great source of protein, biotin, and range of minerals. This sauce will give you a quick, no-stress burst of flavor, and it makes a great addition to your favorite supper.

Serves 6
Preparation time: 10 minutes

1 cup unsalted peanuts

½ cup Vegetable Broth (*see* page 60), plus extra if required

2 garlic cloves, minced

½ teaspoon tamari

2 teaspoons sesame oil

1 to 2 tablespoons coconut nectar

2 tablespoons Alchemist's Sauce (*see* page 70)

2 tablespoons lime juice

1 long red Thai chile (or any type of chile you have on hand), or more to taste

⅓ cup coconut milk

Toast the peanuts in a dry skillet over medium heat until lightly toasted.

Place the nuts and all the other ingredients in a food processor. Blend until they are well combined, adjusting the flavor as desired.

The sauce thickens on its own. If you are making this ahead of time and it becomes a little too thick, mix in a little extra broth before serving.

Store in an airtight container in the refrigerator for 3 to 4 days, or freeze.

Sweet Potato Cakes with Almond Butter Sauce

GF VG

These delicious sweet potato cakes are a firm favorite and one of our best-sellers in the restaurant. This is a quick and easy recipe loaded with protein and fiber, and packed full of vitamins and minerals, including vitamins A and C, and potassium. These little potato cakes make great finger food to snack on during the day, or to enjoy sharing as an appetizer. Ideal for picnics and lunchboxes.

Serves 4
Preparation time: 20 minutes, plus cooking quinoa

For the potato cakes
9oz sweet potato, peeled and cut into large cubes
½ cup quinoa, soaked (*see* page 51)
2 tablespoons lemon juice
handful of fresh parsley, finely chopped
½ teaspoon paprika
pinch of salt and pepper
3 tablespoons brown rice flour
½ cup sesame seeds
coconut oil for frying

For the almond butter sauce
2 tablespoons almond butter
1 tablespoon Dijon mustard
1½ tablespoons lemon juice
½ to 1 cup water

To serve
Green Sauce (*see* page 66), optional

Put the sweet potatoes into a saucepan of boiling water and cook until they are soft enough to break with a fork.

Cook the quinoa (*see* page 5), allow it to cool, and set aside. (We use a rice cooker to do this; if you do this add 1 cup of liquid per cup of quinoa.)

In a large bowl mix together all the ingredients except the rice flour and sesame seeds. Shape the mixture into round cakes (this recipe will yield about 16 to 20 cakes), using the rice flour to shape them and create a nonstick coating. Dredge in the sesame seeds and chill in the refrigerator to set for a couple of hours.

When set, cook the potato cakes in coconut oil in a skillet over medium-low heat until golden brown and a little crisp on both sides.

To make the almond butter sauce, combine all the ingredients in bowl and mix until smooth.

Serve with the potato cakes and drizzle a little Green Sauce over the top, if liked.

Eggplant Rolls with Green Sauce

GF NF VG

Serves 8

Preparation time: 45 minutes, plus 2 hours soaking

For the eggplant rolls
2 large, pear-shaped eggplants, cut lengthwise into ½-inch slices

salt

olive oil

For the sunflower seed pâté
1 cup sunflower seeds, soaked for 2 hours, then drained

¼ cup Vegetable Broth (*see* page 60), plus extra if needed

2 tablespoons tahini

¼ to ⅓ cup lemon juice

1 teaspoon apple cider vinegar

pinch of nutmeg

4 basil leaves

chile flakes (optional)

salt and pepper, to taste

For the lettuce filling
2½ cups corn salad or arugula leaves

1½ tablespoons lemon juice

1½ tablespoons olive oil

To garnish
Green Sauce (*see* page 66)

This is our plant-based version of a sushi roll. Choose the pear-shaped variety of eggplant for this dish because the shape is better for rolling. This recipe is a great source of essential fatty acids, and provides plenty of protein. It is also is nut-free, easy to digest, and full of flavor. Beautiful nourishing finger food that looks gorgeous on the plate.

Lay the eggplant slices on a plate and salt them for about 1 hour until the water has seeped out of them.

Preheat the oven to 475°F.

Wipe the slices dry with paper towels and place on a nonstick baking pan. Bake in the oven for 5 to 7 minutes, turning once, until the slices start turning brown. They should be golden and cooked through, but not mushy. Handle them with care; they will be the outer wrapping of the sushi.

To make the sunflower seed pâté, put the ingredients in a blender and blitz at high speed until they become a creamy, spreadable mixture. If the mixture is too dry, add more vegetable broth until you have the right texture.

Sprinkle the corn salad or arugula leaves with lemon juice, salt, and a little olive oil and toss to coat.

To assemble the rolls, spread a thin layer of pâté along the length of an eggplant slice. Take a few leaves and place them at the narrower end of the slice. Start rolling from this end toward the wider end.

Repeat with all the eggplant slices, then place them on a plate seam-side down so that the leaves come out of both ends. Top the eggplant rolls with a drizzle of green sauce. Serve at room temperature or deliciously cold.

Okra Caponata

Inspired by the Sicilian classic recipe, this dish replaces eggplant with okra and adds some flavors that take it to new heights. Okra is rich in vitamins and minerals and supplies healthy doses of calcium, iron, magnesium, potassium, and zinc. It's great for fiber, too. The turmeric has bioactive compounds with powerful medicinal properties, and is anti-inflammatory and high in antioxidants. Great served hot, cold, or at room temperature, this tastes even better the next day.

Serves 6

Preparation time: 10 minutes, plus 16 minutes cooking

½ onion, chopped

1 celery stalk, leaves attached, chopped

2 tablespoons coconut oil, divided

1lb 2oz okra, chopped into ½-inch slices

1 teaspoon ground turmeric

1 garlic clove, chopped

1½ cups chopped fresh tomatoes

1 tablespoon capers

8 black olives, pitted and halved

2 tablespoons apple cider vinegar

2 teaspoons coconut nectar

salt

Place the onion and the celery in a saucepan with 1 tablespoon of the coconut oil and sauté over low heat until translucent. Add the okra and another tablespoon of coconut oil and sauté for 6 to 8 minutes.

Add the turmeric and garlic and sauté for a further minute. Add the tomatoes, stir, and cover the saucepan. Reduce the heat to very low and cook for 6 minutes, or until the okra is tender.

Remove from the heat and add the capers, olives, vinegar, and coconut nectar. Stir and check the seasoning. This dish can be served hot, at room temperature, or refrigerator cold.

Cauliflower Nuggets

These cauliflower nuggets have the wonderfully crunchy texture that is usually the result of breading and frying. Fun to eat and great to share, try them as a quick eat-and-go snack, or serve with drinks as a pre-dinner nibble with friends.

Serves 6

Preparation time: 25 minutes, plus 30 minutes baking

1 medium head cauliflower, cored and cut into bite-sized florets
1 teaspoon Philosopher's Sauce (*see* page 64)
¼ cup lime juice
1 cup gluten-free rolled oats
½ cup desiccated coconut
1 red chile
1 teaspoon fine salt
1 teaspoon smoked paprika
¼ teaspoon pepper
½ cup hemp seeds
½ cup flaxseeds
½ cup poppy seeds
½ cup black sesame seeds
½ cup almond butter
1 tablespoon lemon juice
small handful of cilantro, chopped

Preheat the oven to 400°F. Line a large baking pan with nonstick parchment paper.

Mix the cauliflower florets in the Philosopher's Sauce and lime juice and let marinate for about 20 minutes.

In a food processor, blend the oats, coconut, chile, salt, paprika, and black pepper until they have a mealy texture. Do not over-process or make the texture too fine; you need a coarse texture.

Add all the seeds, stir, and transfer the mixture to a shallow bowl for dredging.

Thin the almond butter with ¼ cup water and the lemon juice to create a batter. If it's too thick, add a little more water to give you a creamy texture.

Dip the florets into the batter, dredge in the oatmeal and seed coating, and place on the prepared baking pan.

Bake in the oven for 30 minutes. Remove from the oven, sprinkle with the chopped cilantro, and serve in a beautiful bowl.

Wild Teff Wraps with Mushroom Filling

Serves 6

Preparation time: 20 minutes, plus 5 minutes cooking

For the wraps

¾ cup teff flour

1 cup water

½ teaspoon ground turmeric

½ teaspoon cracked peppercorns

salt

olive oil, for frying

For the sprout salad

⅓ cup lentil sprouts (*see* page 53)

⅓ cup fenugreek sprouts (*see* page 53)

⅓ cup olive oil

⅓ cup lemon juice

¼ teaspoon salt

¼ teaspoon coconut nectar

For the mushrooms

3½oz shiitake mushrooms, sliced

2 tablespoons sesame oil

1 garlic clove, grated

1 teaspoon Philosopher's Sauce (*see* page 64)

2 tablespoons lime juice

salt

To serve

Satay Sauce (*see* page 117)

3oz arugula, chopped, salted, and lightly oiled

1 tablespoon toasted pumpkin seeds

Teff is one of the smallest grains in the world, similar in size to a poppy seed. It's the most nutritious of all the grains, with a high fiber content and is a great source of protein, manganese, iron, and calcium. Teff also acts as a probiotic. This healthy wrap is served with nutritious sprouts. It's light to eat and very tasty.

Mix together all the ingredients for the wraps. This batter may seem a little watery, but that is intentional. Set aside.

Make the salad by mixing the sprouts together. Put the rest of the ingredients into a screw-top jar, seal the lid securely, and shake vigorously. Pour evenly over the sprouts and set aside.

Sauté the mushrooms in the sesame oil in a skillet over high heat. When seared on one side, add the garlic, Philosopher's Sauce, lime juice, and salt. Stir, remove from the heat, and put into a dish.

Make the wraps in a heavy nonstick skillet. Add enough oil to just cover the bottom of the pan. Pour 2 tablespoons of batter into the center of the pan. Let it spread out so the wrap is as thin as possible and holds its shape. Cook it until the top is no longer wet and the wrap has a lacy appearance. Carefully flip it over and cook for a further minute. Aim for a wrap size of 3¼ to 4 inches. You may have to test one or two to get the skillet to the right cooking temperature. Repeat until you have used up all the batter.

To assemble, take a wrap and spread it with Satay Sauce. Top with arugula, sprout salad, mushrooms, and some toasted pumpkin seeds.

Note

Use a good-quality skillet made of nontoxic material that cooks well at high temperatures to prevent the wraps from sticking. The Kitchen Equipment section (*see* page 46–8) gives more information on pans.

Chickpea Popcorn

This crunchy, spicy take on popcorn is perfect for party nibbles, movie snacks, taking to the beach, or adding to a lunchbox. These add high levels of fiber, protein, iron, and zinc to your diet. Choose small chickpeas for and be sure to make plenty. Ideal for sharing.

Serves 4
Preparation time: 5 minutes

3 cups cooked chickpeas
  (the smallest you can find)
2 tablespoons olive oil
1½ teaspoons Farmacy Seed Mix
  (*see* page 80)
1 teaspoon smoked paprika
½ teaspoon salt

Preheat the oven to 400°F.

Put all the ingredients in a large bowl and toss until the chickpeas are well coated.

Place on a baking pan and bake in the middle of the oven until crisp. This usually takes about 50 minutes.

Soups are a perfect way to get a hit of nutrients with maximum taste and versatility. Each soup in this collection is a special combination with a unique taste. All are easy to make in advance to keep eating well as part of a busy lifestyle. The salads give a powerful punch of taste, color, nutrition, and vibrancy. Food that is good to eat anytime, across the seasons.

Soups & Salads

Farm Green Soup

This soup is a Farmacy classic that has a wonderful depth of taste and delivers fiber, healthy fats, protein, and a range of vitamins in one delicious bowl of goodness. The watercress contains vitamin C, more calcium than milk, more iron than spinach, and more folate than bananas. In the winter, serve the soup warm with a dash of olive oil. In the summer, serve it cold with a spoonful of Farmacy Cashew Yogurt.

Serves 4

Preparation time: 15 to 20 minutes, plus soaking time

1 tablespoon cold-pressed coconut oil

1 leek, chopped

2 garlic cloves, chopped

1 large head of broccoli, cut into bite-sized pieces, stem peeled and chopped

3¾ cups Vegetable Broth (*see* page 60), plus extra if needed

1 teaspoon salt

7oz Swiss chard, stems removed (keep the stems for Mushrooms and Chard Stems with Tarragon Sauce—*see* page 190)

3½oz watercress

1 teaspoon spirulina

½ very ripe avocado

1½ tablespoons lemon juice

¼ cup almonds, soaked (optional, *see* page 49)

To garnish

toasted pumpkin seeds

sprouts

Cashew Yogurt (*see* page 76)

olive oil, to drizzle

Put the coconut oil into a heavy saucepan over medium heat and sauté the leek until soft. Add the garlic and sauté for a further minute.

Add the broccoli, broth, and salt and bring to a boil. Reduce the heat and simmer for 5 minutes. Add the chard and cook for a further 5 minutes.

Remove the pan from the heat and stir in the watercress and spirulina. Let the soup cool slightly, then transfer to a blender with the avocado, lemon juice, and soaked almonds, if using. Blend until smooth. The longer it's processed, the smoother the soup will become. If it's too thick, add more stock until it becomes creamy.

Garnish with toasted pumpkin seeds, sprouts, Cashew Yogurt, and a swirl of olive oil.

Celestial Purple Soup

This is one of Camilla's special recipes—a simple soup with a beautiful color—that she loves to make for friends. Cauliflower is one of the most nutritious of the cruciferous vegetables and is high in vitamin C and other vitamins, and minerals. It's anti-inflammatory, detoxifying, antioxidant-rich, and a booster for brain and heart health. This stunning soup is ideal served as a delicious lunch or appetizer.

Serves 8

Preparation time: 4 minutes, plus 25 minutes cooking and 2 minutes blending

1½ cups coarsely chopped leeks

1 tablespoon olive oil, plus extra for garnish

1¼ cups cauliflower florets

1 quart Vegetable Broth
(*see* page 60), divided

1¼lb red cabbage, sliced

¼ cup almonds, soaked overnight
(*see* page 49)

½ cup almond milk

salt

To garnish

Cashew Yogurt (*see* page 76)

beet sprouts

In a heavy saucepan, sauté the leeks in the olive oil for about 3 minutes until soft. Add the cauliflower and ½ cup of the Vegetable Broth to the pan and cook until the cauliflower is almost cooked through; about 10 minutes.

Add the red cabbage and stir, making sure it is coated with the liquid. Cook for about 5 minutes, then reduce the heat to medium and add the rest of the Vegetable Broth. Turn off the heat and let stand for 20 minutes until cooled.

Put the mixture into a food processor with the drained almonds and almond milk and blend until very smooth.

Garnish with a swirl of olive oil, some cashew yogurt, and a scattering of beet sprouts.

Kitchari Soup

This is a deeply nourishing soup fortified with sprouts, kale, and turmeric. The combination creates a taste sensation. The sprouts in this dish are high in life-force energy and are anti-inflammatory, while the turmeric and nutrient-dense kale are loaded with antioxidants. This is delicious in any season and can be served hot or cold. We know we shouldn't have favorites, but we do. This is one of them.

Serves 6

Preparation time: 40 minutes, plus sprouting time

3 tablespoons olive oil

½ onion, chopped

3 tablespoons chopped celery

small handful of cilantro stems, finely chopped

2 garlic cloves, finely chopped

2 teaspoons Farmacy Seed Mix (*see* page 80)

1 teaspoon ground turmeric

4½oz kale, chopped

2⅔ cups Vegetable Broth (*see* page 60) or water, divided

2¼ cups sprouted mung beans (*see* page 53)

1¼ cups coconut milk

½ cup tomatoes, seeded and chopped

2 tablespoons coconut nectar

2 tablespoons Philosopher's Sauce (*see* page 64)

salt and pepper

cilantro leaves, to garnish

In a large saucepan, heat the olive oil and add the onion, celery, and cilantro stems. Cook for 3 minutes.

Add the garlic, seed mix, and turmeric and cook for another minute. Add the kale with ½ cup of the Vegetable Broth or water and simmer for 5 minutes.

Next, add the mung beans, the rest of the Vegetable Broth, salt, and pepper. Stir well to combine. Cook until the beans are almost tender, about 10 minutes.

Add the coconut milk, tomatoes, coconut nectar, and Philosopher's Sauce and let simmer for another 10 minutes.

When the beans are ready, taste and adjust the salt as needed.

Garnish with the cilantro leaves.

Note

This soup is like a stew and has a chunky texture. Be careful to avoid adding too much liquid.

136 SOUPS & SALADS

Mexican Soup

Serves 6 to 8
Preparation time: 30 minutes

1 tablespoon coconut oil

½ red onion, diced

6 cilantro sprigs, stems chopped,
   leaves to garnish

1 red bell pepper, thinly sliced

1¾oz celery leaves, chopped

3 garlic cloves, finely chopped

1½ tablespoons paprika (sweet or smoked)

1 tablespoon ground cumin

2 teaspoons chopped oregano leaves

1 cup chopped tomatoes

1 to 2 red chiles, finely chopped (optional)

3 cups Vegetable Broth (*see* page 60), divided

4 cups peeled and diced sweet potato

1 cup cooked chickpeas

2 to 3 tablespoons coconut nectar

¼ cup lime juice

salt

To garnish

cubed avocado

toasted pumpkin seeds

roasted tomato skins, chopped (*see* page 140),
   optional

coconut yogurt

This hearty soup is perfect for getting cozy on cold days. It is inspired by an Aztec recipe called *pozole*. This is traditionally a ceremonial stew flavored with a combination of New World foods such as sweet bell peppers from Mexico, smoked paprika, tomatoes, and the Inca sweet potato. This version includes celery leaves, rich in vitamin E and calcium, and a variety of vegetables and spices that deliver vitamins and minerals. The cilantro stems and leaves support toxic metal cleansing. A warm, nourishing dish with a deep flavor.

In a heavy saucepan heat the coconut oil over medium-high heat and add the onion, cilantro stems, and bell pepper. Sauté for about 5 minutes until translucent and soft. Add the celery leaves and garlic and sauté for 1 minute.

Add the paprika (use smoked for a deeper flavor) and the cumin and cook with the vegetables for 1 to 2 minutes, taking care not to burn the spices.

Add the oregano with the tomatoes and the chiles (if using) and cook for another 5 minutes, stirring regularly, until you have a deep red vegetable base. Add 2 cups of the Vegetable Broth, reserving 1 cup for later. Bring to a boil.

Add the sweet potato and simmer for 10 minutes, until it is soft but not mushy.

Add the chickpeas and coconut nectar and cook for 2 more minutes. Season with salt, remove from the heat, and cover. The soup will be a chunky broth at this stage. Add some of the reserved Vegetable Broth if more liquid is needed and adjust the seasoning.

Before serving, add the lime juice. Garnish with avocado cubes, toasted pumpkin seeds, chopped tomato skins, cilantro leaves, and coconut yogurt.

Roasted Tomato Soup

This is one of Pietro's favorite recipes. He created it with ingredients fresh from the garden. It's a classic tomato soup with a Farmacy twist designed to extract as much flavor as possible from the tomatoes. Tomatoes are one of nature's great umami offerings and roasting them intensifies their flavor. The challenge is to make a tomato soup that doesn't taste like tomato sauce. We've mixed it up and added some favorite ingredients to create a big-flavor, classic recipe. The tomato skins are used as they contain nutritional gems and this adds to the deep flavor of the soup. Serve cold gazpacho style, or warm with a spoonful of Farmacy Cashew Yogurt.

Serves 4

Preparation time: 5 minutes,
   plus 4 hours roasting

12 medium tomatoes, halved

3 tablespoons nutritional yeast

2 tablespoons cashews

2 black garlic cloves, left whole

¼ cup almond milk

1 tablespoon Alchemist's Sauce (*see* page 70)

2 cups Vegetable Broth (*see* page 60)

To garnish

sprouts or microgreens

Cashew Yogurt (*see* page 76)

olive oil, for drizzling

Preheat the oven to 250°F. Place the tomato halves cut-side down on a baking pan lined with nonstick parchment paper. Roast in the oven for 2 hours.

Remove the baking pan from the oven, peel the tomatoes, and place the skins in an ovenproof dish. Remove the paper from the baking pan, turn the tomatoes over to expose the cut sides and return them to the oven alongside the skins.

Roast for a further 2 hours, then remove from the oven and let cool.

Mince the tomato skins using a knife or blitz them in a small food processor until they become almost salt-like and set aside.

Place the tomato flesh in a food processor with the nutritional yeast, cashews, garlic, almond milk, Alchemist's Sauce, and the Vegetable Broth and blend until very smooth.

Serve garnished with the tomato skins, sprouts or microgreens, Cashew Yogurt, and a swirl of olive oil.

Note

If your tomatoes are not quite ripe enough, add 1 tablespoon of coconut nectar to bolster the sweetness.

Sea Mineral & Mushroom Soup

The combination of seaweed and shiitake mushrooms in this dish gives you a strong boost of vitamins and minerals. There is so much goodness in every bowl. We would happily eat this every day.

Serves 6

Preparation time: 10 minutes, plus 10 minutes cooking

1 onion, thinly sliced

½ tablespoon sesame oil

1 garlic clove, crushed

1 tablespoon lime juice, divided

1 teaspoon coconut nectar

10½oz fresh shiitake mushrooms, sliced

5½oz other mushrooms (such as cremino, oyster, or portobello), sliced

1 quart warm water, or 1 quart Seaweed Broth (*see* page 61) and 1 quart Vegetable Broth (*see* page 60)

2 tablespoons tamari

2¼oz dried mixed seaweed, soaked for 5 minutes

2 tablespoons grated ginger root

1 tablespoon rice vinegar

salt and freshly ground white pepper

In a heavy saucepan sauté the onion in the sesame oil until almost brown, being careful not to burn it.

Add the garlic and stir. Pour in half the lime juice and all the coconut nectar and mix. Add the mushrooms and a pinch of salt and sauté for about 4 minutes.

Add the water or broth, if using, along with the tamari. Bring to a boil, remove from the heat, and add the seaweed, ginger, and rice vinegar. Adjust the seasoning with salt, pepper, and lime juice.

Serve in beautiful bowls.

Green Salad with Lentil Dressing GF NF VG

This is a crowd pleaser that gets rave reviews whenever we serve it. Good for healthy fiber intake, this salad contains iron and supports the heart. We prefer not to use a lot of oil in our recipes and here we replace oil with a well-flavored lentil sauce to create a protein-rich, nutritious salad. It's a simple dish to assemble, using ingredients already prepared from the Basics chapter (*see* page 58). The lentil dressing can be served cold in the summer or warm in winter and works as a healthy feast either way.

Serves 4
Preparation time: 10 minutes

1½ tablespoons Dijon mustard

1 tablespoon Farmacy Seed Mix (*see* page 80)

dash of tamari

1½ tablespoons lemon juice, divided

⅓ cup Vegetable Broth (*see* page 60)

1 cup cooked green lentils (*see* page 57 for soaking and cooking)

1 crisp baby Romaine lettuce, or any sturdy greens

¼ teaspoon salt

To garnish

Roasted Red Bell Pepper Confit (*see* page 208)

1 tablespoon Farmacy Seed Mix (*see* page 80)

sprouts

Start by making the dressing. Mix together the mustard, seed mix, tamari, and 1 tablespoon of lemon juice. If the dressing seems too thick, thin it by adding a little Vegetable Broth. Stir it into the cooked lentils.

Sprinkle the lettuce or greens with salt and a dash of lemon juice. Gently toss the leaves. Arrange them on a plate and top with the dressed lentils and roasted bell pepper strips. Garnish with the seed mix and sprouts.

Note

This dish works well using green lentils because they have a specific cooking time, a unique taste, and a creamy consistency that is ideal here. We don't recommend using other type of lentils for this recipe.

Roasted Carrot & Avocado Salad

This salad includes the surprise combination of carrot and avocado. The mixture of flavors and textures work so well together that it has become one of our favorite dishes to make for friends. Chia seeds are used to emulsify the dressing. This pretty, colorful salad is rich in fatty acids and vitamins and has an additional protein boost from the hazelnuts.

Serves 4

Preparation time: 10 minutes, plus 35 minutes roasting

12 to 16 baby carrots

1½ tablespoons Farmacy Seed Mix (*see* page 80)

3 tablespoons lime juice

3 tablespoons olive oil

1 teaspoon sherry vinegar

1 red chile

good pinch of salt

2 teaspoons chia seeds soaked in Seaweed Broth (*see* page 61)

14oz mixed arugula, mizuna greens, and watercress leaves

1 ripe avocado, cubed

2 tablespoons toasted and chopped hazelnuts

Preheat the oven to 400°F. Rub the carrots with the seed mix and put in a roasting pan. Add ¼ cup of water, cover with nonstick parchment paper, and roast in the oven for about 20 minutes.

Take the pan out of the oven, remove the paper, and return the carrots to the oven to roast for another 30 minutes until nicely caramelized. Remove from the oven and let cool.

Combine the lime juice, olive oil, sherry vinegar, whole chile, pinch of salt, and chia seeds. Whisk together for about a minute to create an emulsion, then set aside. Remove the chile before serving.

In a serving bowl combine the leaves, carrots, and avocado and toss with the emulsion. Serve topped with the hazelnuts.

Fennel & Spinach with Carrot Dressing

GF NF R VG

Here's a dish that captures the fresh flavors of the garden, combining spinach, fresh tomatoes, and zingy fennel. It's packed full of vitamins and minerals, with good levels of fiber, zinc, and calcium. The dressing is part of the family of dressings we create using vegetables as a base. Here, raw carrots combined with brown rice miso transform into a silky, golden sauce. This recipe makes a perfect appetizer and can be doubled for more festive occasions and celebrations.

Serves 4
Preparation time: 15 minutes

For the salad
1 fennel bulb, thinly sliced
½ teaspoon salt
7oz baby spinach
20 cherry tomatoes, halved
toasted hemp seeds, to garnish

For the dressing
1 large carrot, coarsely chopped
⅓ cup water
1½ tablespoons brown rice miso
1 tablespoon lime juice
1 tablespoon white wine vinegar
¼ cup sesame oil
¾-inch piece of fresh ginger root
2 tablespoons maple syrup

Rub the fennel slices with the salt and set aside for 5 minutes.

Make the dressing by putting all the ingredients into a food processor and blending until very smooth. Check for seasoning.

Arrange the salad on a serving plate, garnish with the toasted hemp seeds, and serve with the dressing.

Beet Top Salad

This salad has a style of its own with its blend of intense colors. All parts of the beets are used including the leaves, which are highly perishable and therefore a great indicator of the freshness of the root. This salad tastes even better eaten the next day, as the flavors deepen. The dish is high in zinc and iron and contains protein, fiber, magnesium, potassium, copper, and manganese. Beet greens also supply significant quantities of vitamin A and C, as well as calcium to help bone strength and support the immune system.

Serves 4 to 6

Preparation time: 20 minutes, plus 60 minutes roasting

3 beets (with green tops) plus extra beet tops

3 tablespoons lemon juice, divided

1 tablespoon extra virgin olive oil, divided, plus extra for frying

1 garlic clove, crushed

2 tablespoons tahini

1 tablespoon apple cider vinegar

2 teaspoons coconut nectar

⅓ cup water

½ teaspoon brown rice miso

8 pencil-thin asparagus spears, or 8 thick spears cut diagonally

1 cup cooked buckwheat (*see* page 51)

salt and pepper

To garnish

Cashew Yogurt (*see* page 76)

⅓ cup pomegranate seeds

¼ cup toasted pumpkin seeds

Preheat the oven to 400°F

Cut off the beet tops and set aside. Place the beets on a baking pan lined with nonstick parchment paper and roast on the middle rack of the oven for about 1 hour.

Remove from the oven and, once the beets have cooled a little, peel the skins away with your hands. Cube the beets, dress with a dash of lemon juice and a drizzle of olive oil, and set aside.

To prepare the dressing, infuse the rest of the lemon juice with the crushed garlic. Let stand for 10 minutes. Strain and reserve the infused juice and discard the garlic. Blend together the infused lemon juice, the rest of the olive oil, the tahini, cider vinegar, coconut nectar, water, and miso in a food processor.

Separate the beet leaves from the stems. Heat a skillet over high heat and sauté the leaves in olive oil for 30 seconds, season with salt and pepper, and remove from the pan.

Cut the beet stems into 1¼-inch pieces. Put them in the skillet and sauté until almost charred. Sprinkle with a little salt and taste. Once done, add the asparagus spears and cook until soft, about 5 minutes.

Combine the buckwheat, beet stems, and asparagus, toss with two-thirds of the dressing, and arrange on a serving plate. Toss the leaves with the remaining dressing and place on top of the buckwheat. Drizzle with the Cashew Yogurt, add the cubed beets, and sprinkle with pomegranate and pumpkin seeds.

Note

Beet cubes will stain everything pink, so add them at the end.

Kale & Sprouts with Almond Cream

This salad combines kale and sprouted beans. Kale is one of the great supergreens. It's high in fiber and packed with vitamins. The sprouted beans are full of natural, energy-giving life force and one of the most nutrient-dense sprouting foods. The kale is simmered, creating the perfect texture to mix with the beans. The lemon adds a tangy note, which is a delicious contrast to the almond butter dressing. A great dish served warm on a cold day.

Serves 6

Preparation time: 10 minutes, plus 10 minutes cooking time

2 teaspoons olive oil

2 medium garlic cloves, minced

1 tablespoon grated fresh ginger root

1lb 2oz lacinato kale leaves, coarsely chopped (avoid curlier kale)

½ cup Vegetable Broth (*see* page 60)

1½ cups sprouted mung beans (*see* page 53)

1½ tablespoons lemon juice, or to taste

2 teaspoons tamari, or to taste

For the dressing

2 tablespoons almond butter

1½ tablespoons lemon juice

½ teaspoon salt

¼ cup water

Heat the olive oil in a heavy saucepan over medium heat and briefly sauté the garlic and ginger.

Add the kale leaves and toss before adding the broth. Bring to a boil, reduce the heat, and cover the pan. Simmer for 5 minutes.

Add the mung beans and simmer for another 5 minutes.

Add the lemon juice and tamari to taste. Add more lemon juice if necessary, then remove the kale and mung beans from the heat and let stand for a couple of minutes.

For the dressing, mix the almond butter, lemon juice, and salt in a bowl and slowly add the water. The consistency should be thick and creamy—not runny, but not too stiff either.

Spoon a tablespoon of the dressing onto a serving plate and spread it out to create a thin layer. Pile the kale and mung beans on top.

Note

Do not use unsprouted mung beans, as they will need to cook for 40 minutes, by which time the kale will be overcooked.

Sea Vegetable Salad

Serves 4
Preparation time: 30 minutes

For the cucumber marinade
⅓ cup rice vinegar
1 tablespoon finely chopped dill
¾ teaspoon salt
¾ teaspoon coconut nectar

For the salad
1 large, seedless cucumber, thinly sliced
1 small carrot, sliced into matchsticks
½ teaspoon salt
3oz dried green mixed seaweed
2¼oz daikon radish, thinly sliced
1 small bunch of watercress
1 lime
2 tablespoons dry toasted black sesame seeds
1 nori sheet

For the dressing
1 cup tahini
½ cup rice vinegar
¼ cup olive oil
2 tablespoons toasted sesame oil
2 tablespoons grated fresh ginger root
¼ cup lemon juice
2 tablespoons tamari
½ tablespoon wasabi powder or dried red
  chile flakes (optional)
3 tablespoons coconut nectar

This salad is inspired by Asian flavors and packed full of nutrient-dense ingredients. The peppery watercress provides a burst of vitamins and is one of the power-greens that helps boost immunity and provide high levels of calcium. The mixed seaweed contains minerals and has more nutritional value than any land vegetable. A delicious, zingy salad to pep up your taste buds. Eat this and be strong!

Mix together the cucumber marinade ingredients, pour it over the cucumber slices, and let marinate for at least 30 minutes.

Rub ½ teaspoon of salt into the carrot sticks and set aside.

Put the mixed seaweed into a large bowl and cover with cold water. Let stand for 5 to 10 minutes to soak until softened. Drain in a colander, pat dry, and place in a serving bowl. Make sure it is completely dry and not holding excess moisture.

Make the dressing by combining all the ingredients in a high-speed blender to form a thick, creamy consistency; this will be the base of the dish. Spoon a tablespoon or so of the dressing onto the serving platter.

Mix the seaweed, carrot, daikon radish, and watercress together. Squeeze lime juice over them. Taste and add salt if necessary.

Place the seaweed-watercress mixture in a mound in the center of a bowl. Thin the dressing with a little water and drizzle it over the greens. Top with the marinated cucumber and drizzle with the remaining dressing.

Finish the dish by sprinkling it with the toasted black sesame seeds, then cut the nori sheet into ribbons and place on top.

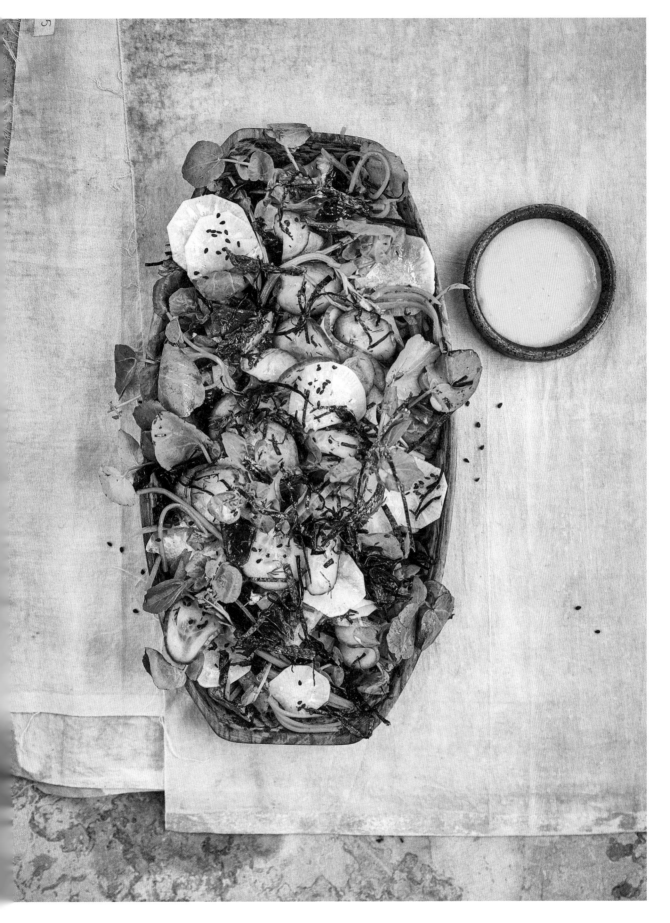

Farmacy Caesar Salad

GF VG

Caesar salad is one of the greatest dishes when made well. It's hard to find a version that is truly plant-based, but we think this recipe nails the challenge well. This dish has been given the Farmacy makeover, combining olives, capers, and lemons with our deep-tasting Alchemist's Sauce, creating a uniquely zesty Caesar dressing. It's completely oil-free, too. This dish works well as an appetizer or a main. It's a light, healthy salad that delivers on nutrition, with the Seaweed Broth and fresh green leaves providing a good-looking lunch or supper dish.

Serves 4
Preparation time: 15 minutes

For the Caesar dressing
3 tablespoons lemon juice
1 garlic clove, crushed
7 Kalamata olives, pitted
1 tablespoon capers
1 teaspoon lemon zest
1 tablespoon Alchemist's Sauce
  (*see* page 70)
1 tablespoon Philosopher's Sauce
  (*see* page 64)
1 teaspoon Dijon mustard
3 tablespoons almond butter
2½ tablespoons nutritional yeast
3 tablespoons water

To serve
leaves of 1 baby Romaine lettuce
Alchemist's Sauce (*see* page 70)
lemon juice
chopped parsley
pepper

To make the dressing, add the crushed garlic to the lemon juice and allow to infuse for 10 minutes. Strain and discard the garlic.

Place all the dressing ingredients in a food processor except the almond butter, water, and yeast. Process until smooth; about 10 seconds. Mix in the almond butter and water until you have a consistency like mayonnaise; this takes about 4 minutes. Pour into a bowl and finish by mixing in the nutritional yeast by hand.

To serve, mix the lettuce leaves with a little Alchemist's Sauce and lemon juice and toss lightly. Add the dressing slowly until you have a good balance of leaves and dressing.

Finish the salad with chopped parsley and freshly ground pepper.

White Bean Salad

This had to be included in the salads that made the cut as it's one of our favorite dishes of all time. It's a light-tasting salad that's filling, too. It's quick to make once the beans are cooked. Even our friends who say they don't like white beans changed their minds after eating this. Everyone seems to love it—bean lovers and nonbean lovers alike. During the tasting sessions, more than one taster said afterwards, "That was one of my favorite dishes, and I thought I didn't like white beans!" It's a protein-rich recipe that gives an added boost of vitamin A. The apple cider vinegar helps digestion.

Serves 4

Preparation time: 5 minutes, plus bean preparation

1 carrot, diced

2 celery stalks, chopped

¾ cup coarsely chopped arugula

3 cups cooked lima beans

green part of a scallion, thinly sliced

1 tablespoon Farmacy Seed Mix (*see* page 80)

2 tablespoons sherry vinegar

1 tablespoon apple cider vinegar

3 tablespoons olive oil

2 large ripe tomatoes, quartered, seeds removed, flesh cubed

salt

Green Sauce (*see* page 66)

Place the carrot, celery, arugula, and lima beans in a mixing bowl. Season with sliced scallion, the seed mix, 1 tablespoon of the sherry vinegar, the apple cider vinegar, and the olive oil. Mix and let rest for at least 1 hour.

Season the tomato with salt and the remaining sherry vinegar.

To serve, pile the lima bean mixture into a single mound. Make a ring around the mound with the tomato cubes. Garnish with small drops of Green Sauce.

The Farmacy earth bowls are a centerpiece of our food story, a one-world concept in which we use the best flavors we can gather from all corners of this beautiful planet. These are all dishes in which a blend of flavors is served in one big bowl.

Earth Bowls

What is an Earth Bowl?

The ingredients in each of our earth bowls are carefully selected and combined to be health-supporting and delicious. Each recipe includes a gluten-free grain and three or four dishes combined to create a spectacular harmony of taste, color, and nutritional benefit. All the bowls come with a sauce to bind all of the ingredients together and are topped with fresh sprouts and/or seeds, which add goodness and color to the dish. The recipes that follow in this section show how to make distinctive earth bowls, and you can have fun creating a look that you love using a vibrant palette of different colors, tastes, and textures.

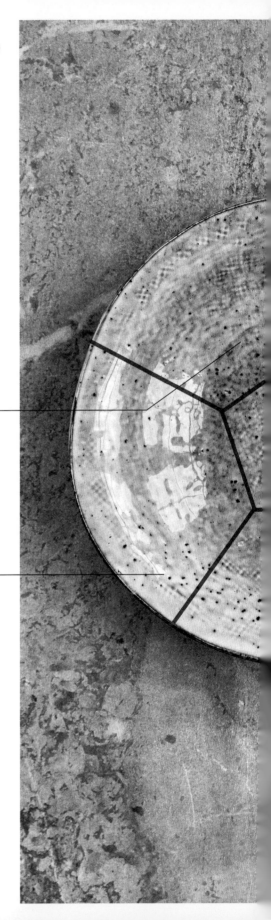

Healthy fats

Avocado

Dried coconut

Nuts—almonds, cashews, walnuts, pecans

Seeds—sunflower, pumpkin, hemp, sesame

Raw items

Arugula

Asparagus

Beets

Carrot

Cucumber

Fennel

Herbs

Radishes

Salad leaves

Seaweed

Sprouts

Tomatoes

Watercress

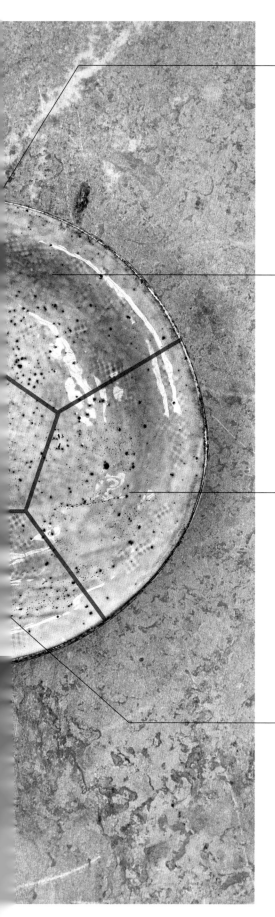

Base

Grain—rice, millet
Kale
Leafy greens
Noodle—rice noodle, soba noodle
Seed—buckwheat, quinoa

Carbohydrate

Celery root
Lotus root
Potatoes
Sweet potato

Cooked vegetables

Bell peppers
Broccoli
Brussels sprouts
Cauliflower
Eggplant
Kale
Spinach
Zucchini

Legume

Black beans
Chickpeas
Falafels
Lentils
Mung beans

Farmacy Macro Bowl

Serves 4

**Preparation time: 30 minutes, plus
    20 minutes cooking**

For the salad

olive oil, for roasting and dressing

2¼lb sweet potatoes, cut into
    ¾-inch cubes

1 head of broccoli, cut into bite-sized pieces

2 avocados, chopped into chunks

juice of 1 lime

½oz dried seaweed mix, soaked
    in warm water

3½oz mixed greens (corn salad, arugula,
    and watercress)

1 cup mixed sprouts (radish, broccoli,
    and fenugreek)

juice of ½ lemon

1¼ cups cooked quinoa (*see* page 51)

salt and black pepper

For the dressing

1 large zucchini, peeled, chopped, and seeded

1 tablespoon lemon juice

⅓ cup Cashew Yogurt (*see* page 76)

1 tablespoon Alchemist's Sauce (*see* page 70)

¼ cup nutritional yeast

2 teaspoons chia seeds

3 pitted dates, soaked for 30 minutes

3 tablespoons tamari

¼ cup Vegetable Broth (*see* page 60)

1 chile

3 tablespoons chopped tarragon leaves

This Farmacy classic is a nourishing bowl with a focus on sea and land vegetables, including sweet potato, seaweed, and broccoli, that has quinoa at its heart. This satisfying meal will have you feeling wonderfully well-fed and ensure you leave the table feeling energized. An everyday dish that gives you all you want in a bowl and provides a broad range of nutrients the body needs, including protein, vitamins, minerals, and iron.

Preheat the oven to 400°F.

To prepare the salad, pour some olive oil into a baking pan, add the sweet potato cubes, and roast for 20 minutes until cooked through, or longer if necessary. Sprinkle with salt and set aside.

Steam or boil the broccoli until al dente; about 6 minutes. Drain and dress with a little oil and salt.

Dress the avocado chunks with lime juice and salt and set aside.

Drain the seaweed and pat dry thoroughly. Dress with a little olive oil and salt.

Combine the greens and sprouts and dress with lemon juice.

Make the dressing by placing all the ingredients in a food processor and blending until smooth.

To assemble, pile a small mound of the quinoa in the center of the bowl and arrange the sweet potato, greens and sprouts, avocado, seaweed, and broccoli around it. Stir the dressing well and serve alongside the salad.

Kimchi Bowl

NF VG

Serves 4
**Preparation time: 30 minutes, plus
20 minutes cooking**

6 spears white asparagus, peeled and cut
into matchsticks
2 carrots, cut into matchsticks
7oz soba noodles
13oz Kimchi (*see* page 204)
1oz sprout mix
lemon juice, to season

For the mushrooms
1lb 2oz shiitake mushrooms
¼ cup sesame oil, plus extra for the noodles
¼ cup rice vinegar
1 garlic clove, left whole
2 teaspoons coconut nectar
handful of basil leaves
salt and black pepper, to taste

For the spinach stems
stems of ½lb spinach (choose
stems attached to the root)
2 tablespoons coconut oil
1 garlic clove, minced
1 chile, minced
1¾oz fresh dill weed (stems and leaves),
chopped
zest and juice of 1 lime

For the dressing
3 garlic cloves, grated
2 tablespoons grated fresh ginger root
2 tablespoons coconut nectar
2 chiles
2 tablespoons brown rice miso
3 tablespoons sesame oil
3 tablespoons rice vinegar
2 tablespoons lime juice
zest of 1 orange
1 tablespoon Alchemist's Sauce (*see* page 70)
½ teaspoon dried red chile flakes

This is a colorful kimchi and mushroom bowl with a soba noodle base. The spinach stems and dill are inspired by Turkish cooking and mixed with Korean-inspired fermented cabbage. The combination of flavors is delightful. This bowl has a broad range of vitamins and minerals and leaves you feeling good after eating it. The kimchi helps support gut health and good digestion. This bowl is served cold and makes a stunning summer lunch or supper dish.

Season the asparagus matchsticks with a little lemon juice and soak the carrot matchsticks in water to make them softer.

To prepare the mushrooms sauté the mushrooms in the sesame oil in a skillet over high heat until cooked but firm. In a large bowl, combine the mushrooms, vinegar, garlic, coconut nectar, and basil and season with salt and pepper to taste.

Next sauté the spinach in the coconut oil in a skillet over high heat until soft; about 10 minutes. Add the garlic, chile, chopped dill weed, and lemon zest and juice. Season with salt and set aside.

Make the dressing by placing all the ingredients in a food processor and blending until smooth. Season with salt and set aside.

Season the sprout mix with lemon juice and set aside.

Cook the noodles following the package directions. Rinse them in cold water to prevent them from sticking together and run your fingers through them to remove excess starch. Drizzle the noodles with some sesame oil, toss, and set aside.

To assemble, create a small mound of soba noodles on one side of the serving dish. Arrange the asparagus, drained carrots, kimchi, mushrooms, sprouts, and spinach around it. Spoon the dressing over the noodles and enjoy!

166 EARTH BOWLS

Kitchari Bowl

Serves 4
Preparation time: 30 minutes

2 cups white basmati rice, cooked
sprouts, to garnish
1 quantity Cucumber Raita (*see* page 180)

For the mung beans
1 onion, diced
1 mild green chile, cut into strips
2 tablespoons olive oil
2 celery stalks, cut into ¾-inch pieces
2 garlic cloves, chopped
1 small green chile, thinly sliced (optional)
½-inch piece of fresh ginger root, grated
1½ tablespoons ground turmeric
2 tablespoons Farmacy Seed Mix
  (*see* page 80)
2 tomatoes, cut into chunks
½ cup split yellow mung beans, cooked

For the cauliflower
1 teaspoons mild curry powder
1lb 2oz cauliflower, cut into 1-inch florets
1 tablespoon lemon juice
3 tablespoons extra virgin olive oil
salt and black pepper

For the mango chutney
1 ripe mango, cubed, liquid reserved
1 tablespoon water
1 tablespoon apple cider vinegar
1 teaspoon coconut nectar
1 red chile, minced

For the greens
7oz arugula
1 avocado, sliced
2 tablespoons shelled pistachios,
  toasted and chopped
2 tablespoons olive oil
2 tablespoons apple cider vinegar
salt and black pepper

This ancient recipe has been given a Farmacy update, creating a classic, comforting dish that delivers a healthy and tasty hit in one bowl. Kitchari is an easily digestible bowl of nourishing ingredients that's gentle on the stomach. We have added a tomato jam and a spiced cauliflower side, enhancing the nutritional value as well as the flavor. The recipe uses split yellow mung beans, which don't have a gassy bean effect. There's protein, fiber, and a healthy hit of vitamins in this vibrant bowl. White rice is recommended for quicker absorption, and is also ideal for detoxing; any good-quality rice will work well in this dish.

To prepare the mung beans, sauté the onion and pepper in olive oil in a skillet over medium heat until translucent. Add the celery, garlic, chile (if using), ginger, turmeric, and seed mix and cook for 1 minute. Add the tomatoes and simmer until the mixture has a jamlike consistency. Remove from the heat, stir in the cooked mung beans, and set aside.

To prepare the cauliflower, preheat the oven to 400°F. Dry toast the curry powder for 1 minute in a hot skillet without oil and set aside.

Put the cauliflower in a roasting pan and season with salt, pepper, the toasted curry powder, and lemon juice. Add 3 tablespoons of olive oil. Roast in the oven for about 15 minutes, stirring once or twice. Set aside and let cool.

To make the chutney, sauté the mango briefly in a skillet in its own liquid and the water until reduced. Add the vinegar, coconut nectar, and chile and cook for 1 minute more. The mix should not be runny. Set aside.

To prepare the greens, mix all the ingredients together.

Assemble the bowl by piling a mound of rice in the center and arranging all the side dishes around it. Garnish with sprouts.

Japanese Bowl

GF VG

Serves 4
Preparation time: 25 minutes

For the lotus root
1 lotus root (*see* Notes below) cut
    into ¼-inch thick slices
2 tablespoons olive oil
salt

For the almond miso sauce
1 tablespoon brown rice miso
3 tablespoons almond butter
¼ cup fresh apple juice
1 teaspoon maple syrup
½-inch slice of fresh ginger root, grated
¼ cup water

For the spinach
7oz spinach
¼ cup Seaweed Broth (*see* page 61)
1 tablespoon tamari
½ teaspoon coconut nectar
1 tablespoon lime juice

For the beans, seaweed, and asparagus
7oz green beans
12 thin asparagus spears
3½oz mixed seaweed (wakame, dulse, or any
    other ready-to-use seaweed), soaked
1 tablespoon rice vinegar
2 tablespoons lemon juice
2 tablespoons sesame oil,
    plus extra for the noodles
2 tablespoons sesame seeds

9oz black rice noodles
4 radishes, thinly sliced

A bowl inspired by oriental flavors that delivers a powerhouse of nutritional hits from the sprouts, asparagus, and seaweed broth. The apple, ginger, and almond in the sauce give this dish a unique edge and flavor. Raw live sprouts contain good levels of fiber, potassium, copper, and iron. Other important minerals come from the impressive lotus root. This dish is best served cold.

Preheat the oven to 350°F.

Put the lotus root on a baking pan with the oil, season with salt, and bake in the oven for 20 minutes.

Prepare the sauce by mixing all the ingredients together in a bowl. Set aside. If you like, you can adjust the consistency of the sauce later by adding a little more water.

Put the spinach in a small saucepan, add a little boiling water, and cook briefly. Mix the other ingredients to create a dressing. Lightly dress the spinach (you may not need all of the dressing). Set aside.

Boil the beans and the asparagus in separate saucepans until al dente and put them on one side. Drain the seaweed.

Mix the rice vinegar with 1 tablespoon of lemon juice and the sesame oil and add to the beans along with the seaweed. Sprinkle with sesame seeds and set aside. Season the sprouts with the remaining lemon juice.

Cook the noodles following the package directions. Refresh them in cold water and run them through your fingers to remove excess starch. Let cool and then dry and dress lightly with 1 tablespoon of sesame oil.

To assemble, place a small mound of noodles in the bowl. Arrange the beans, spinach, asparagus, and radishes around them. Top with lotus root and some sprouts and serve with the sauce.

Notes

The delicately flavored root of the lotus plant has been popular for centuries in Japan and China. Break the root at the intersections of the individual parts, then wash thoroughly in cold water. Trim the ends and peel off the rough outer skin. Rinse in lemon water (or vinegar) to prevent discoloration.

Mexican Bowl

Serves 4
Preparation time: 20 minutes

1⅓ cups cooked brown rice
1¼ cups chopped cilantro (stems and leaves)
2½ cup dry toasted pumpkin seeds

For the beans
1 tablespoon olive oil
½ onion, diced
1 cup diced red bell pepper
3 tablespoons celery, diced
1 garlic clove, minced
1 small tomato, seeded and diced
3 cups cooked black beans
2 cups Vegetable Broth (*see* page 60)
salt and black pepper

For the avocado and tomato salsa
1 ripe avocado, cubed
2 medium tomatoes, cubed
1 tablespoon apple cider vinegar
1 garlic clove, grated
2 tablespoons chopped cilantro leaves
2 tablespoons lime juice
salt, to season

For the zucchini
1 large zucchini, cubed
1 teaspoon smoked paprika
salt, to season

To garnish
3½oz mixed salad greens
lemon juice, to taste
olive oil
⅓ cup Cashew Yogurt (*see* page 76)
½ cup sprouts
2 tablespoons Farmacy Seed Mix
(*see* page 80)

A best-seller in our restaurant, this is a filling, one-bowl wonder that delivers on taste. We've adapted the recipe to make it easy to prepare at home, while keeping the Mexican-inspired flavors. The beans contain high levels of protein and minerals, there are good fats in the avocado and healthy-gut probiotics in the yogurt. The flavors are deep and satisfying. This remains one of our favorites to savor and enjoy slowly for lunch or supper; a dish to share with some lucky friends.

Make sure the cooked rice is completely cold, then mix with the cilantro and pumpkin seeds. Set aside.

Prepare the beans by sautéing the onion, red bell pepper, celery, and garlic in the olive oil in a heavy saucepan over medium-high heat until the onions are translucent. Add the tomatoes and cook for 1 minute. Add the beans and the Vegetable Broth. Bring to a boil then reduce to a simmer . Cook slowly until greatly reduced, taking care not to let it burn. Season with salt and pepper. Set aside.

For the avocado and the tomato salsa, mix all the ingredients and set aside.

To prepare the zucchini, preheat the oven to 350°F. Place the zucchini cubes on a baking pan, season with paprika and salt, and roast for 10 minutes until al dente.

Dress the mixed salad greens with a splash of lemon juice and a little olive oil and set aside.

Make a mound of rice in the center of a serving dish and place the other dishes around it. Spoon on the cashew yogurt, sprinkle with sprouts and the seed mix, and serve.

Thai Bowl

Serves 4
**Preparation time: 30 minutes, plus
  24 hours pickling**

For the pickled cabbage

1lb 2oz red cabbage, thinly sliced

½ cup apple cider vinegar

¼ cup rice vinegar

2 teaspoons coconut nectar

2 garlic cloves, crushed

2 teaspoons pickling seeds (mustard, fennel,
  coriander, or caraway, or a mixture)

1½ tablespoons salt, plus extra for the
  noodles

black pepper

For the sauce

¼ cup lime juice, plus 2 limes to serve

2 tablespoons Philosopher's Sauce
  (*see* page 64)

2 tablespoons tamarind paste

3 teaspoons coconut nectar

1 tablespoon tamari

1 chile, crushed (optional)

2 garlic cloves, finely chopped

½-inch piece of fresh ginger root, grated

½ cup water

1 tablespoon sesame oil, plus extra for the
  noodles

2 tablespoons almond butter

3 basil leaves, torn

For the vegetables

2 carrots, cut into matchsticks

1 zucchini, cut into matchsticks

1 cup sprouts

4 bok choy, shredded

1 ripe avocado, cubed

11½oz rice noodles

To garnish

cilantro leaves

toasted peanuts

**This bowl is inspired by Thailand's great
national dish, Pad Thai, and the flavors
of the vibrant street food of Bangkok.
The ingredients have anti-inflammatory
properties while the chile and spices aid
digestion and support gut health. Enjoy the
flavors of Asia in this heart-warming bowl.**

Prepare the pickled cabbage a day ahead by sprinkling 1 tablespoon of salt over the cabbage and massaging the salt thoroughly into it. Let rest for half an hour.

Make the pickling liquid by mixing the rest of the ingredients in a large jar with a screw-top lid. Seal securely and shake vigorously until well mixed. Pour the dressing over the cabbage and let marinate for 24 hours.

Transfer the mixture to a clean jar (it should be large enough to hold all of the ingredients with a 1½-inch gap at the top) and refrigerate overnight.

The following day prepare the sauce by mixing together all the ingredients. Set aside.

Prepare the vegetables. Mix together the carrots, zucchini, and sprouts and set aside.

Put the bok choy in a large heatproof bowl and cover with boiling water. Let it stand for a moment, then strain and set aside to cool before combining with the avocado.

Cook the noodles following the package directions. Refresh in cold water and run your fingers through them to wash away the excess starch. Rinse a couple of times in this way, then strain and spread them over a cutting board. As soon as they are dry, dress with 1 tablespoon of sesame oil and sprinkle with salt.

Place a small mound of noodles in the center of the bowl. Add the pickled cabbage, vegetable mix, bok choy, and avocado. Top with roasted peanuts and cilantro leaves. Serve with half a lime for squeezing and the sauce on the side.

Middle Eastern Bowl

Serves 4

Preparation time: 40 minutes, plus
** 15 minutes cooking and refrigeration**

For the millet tabbouleh

2 garlic cloves, minced

zest of ½ lemon

7oz mint leaves, finely chopped

3½oz parsley or arugula, or both

½ cup hazelnuts, toasted then chopped

2 cups cooked millet

1½ teaspoons salt

black pepper

For the cucumber salad

2 cucumbers, chopped

2 garlic cloves, minced

3 tablespoons fresh lemon juice

3 tablespoons olive oil

3 tablespoons chopped cilantro

For the eggplant

5½oz eggplant, sliced

For the tomato salad

2 medium tomatoes, chopped

½-inch slice of lemon, seeded and
  finely chopped

1 teaspoon Farmacy Seed Mix (*see* page 80)

1 tablespoon apple cider vinegar

2 tablespoons chopped cilantro
  (stems and leaves)

For the fattoush dressing

¼ cup olive oil

¼ cup tomato juice

½ teaspoon minced garlic

3 tablespoons lemon juice

1 chile, finely chopped (optional)

To serve

Farmacy Hummus (*see* page 111)

mixed greens

sprouts

This nourishing bowl features the Farmacy version of tabbouleh using millet instead of wheat. The tabbouleh is so delicious that we want to make it constantly just to eat on its own. It tastes even better if refrigerated and eaten the next day (use a little more seasoning if you do this). The fattoush dressing adds a Middle Eastern zing.

Start the tabbouleh. In a bowl, stir together the garlic, lemon zest, mint, parsley or arugula, hazelnuts, salt, and pepper. Set aside.

For the cucumber salad, place the chopped cucumbers on paper towels to dry. Mix the rest of the ingredients to create a dressing. Dress the cucumber pieces and set aside.

Cook the eggplants as described in the Eggplant Steaks recipe (*see* page 186), but skip the salting step. Set aside.

Prepare the tomato salad by mixing all the ingredients. Set aside.

Put all the ingredients for the fattoush dressing into a jar with a screw-top lid, seal securely, and shake vigorously.

Before serving, finish the tabbouleh. Make sure the millet is completely cold so that it will not make the herbs wilt. Combine it with the lemon, herb, and hazelnut mixture using a fork.

Take a serving plate and place a small mound of millet off-center toward the edge of the plate. Place some eggplant, hummus, tomato salad, greens, and cucumber salad around it in a half-moon shape. Top with sprouts and serve with the dressing on the side.

Here's a selection of our favorite main courses, including an adaptation of the famous Farmacy burger. These are dishes to delight in and share, ranging from easy suppers to more elaborate dinner party recipes to eat with friends.

Mains

Sweet Potato & Mushroom Curry

Serves 4

Preparation time: 15 minutes, plus 20 minutes cooking

For the curry paste

1 red chile

4 garlic cloves, coarsely chopped

2 lemon grass stalks, sliced

4 cilantro sprigs, stems included

1½ teaspoons ground turmeric

1 teaspoon salt

For the curry

4 shallots, chopped

4 garlic cloves, chopped

2 tablespoons olive oil

2 tablespoons curry paste (*see* above)

1 tablespoon grated fresh ginger root

2 cups Vegetable Broth (*see* page 60)

2¼lb sweet potatoes, peeled and cubed

2 kaffir lime leaves, chopped

7oz oyster or other mushrooms

¾ cup chopped roasted peanuts

1½ cups coconut milk

3 tablespoons Philosopher's Sauce
   (*see* page 64)

2 tablespoons coconut nectar

For the cucumber raita

2 cucumbers, seeded and diced

½ cup Cashew Yogurt (*see* page 76)

3 tablespoons chopped fresh dill weed

1½ tablespoons lemon juice

To garnish

dry toasted pumpkin seeds

cilantro leaves

2 limes, halved

This Thai-inspired recipe is a homely update on our Farmacy restaurant curry. It's colorful and bursting with goodness. Susie says that this curry would be her desert-island luxury. This is one of the recipes that elicited excited gasps at the testing table. Its flavor is deep and delicious, warming heart and soul.

Blend together all the curry paste ingredients in a food processor until they form a paste. You may need to add a couple tablespoons of water. Set aside. This will make more paste than you need for this recipe, but it will last several months if refrigerated.

To make the curry, sauté the shallots and garlic in the oil in a heavy saucepan over medium heat until they are translucent. Do not let them color. Add the curry paste and ginger and cook for 1 minute.

Add the Vegetable Broth, sweet potatoes, and lime leaves and bring to a boil. Reduce the heat and cook for 10 minutes.

Then add the mushrooms, the peanuts, and the coconut milk. Stir in the Philosopher's Sauce and the coconut nectar. Let simmer for 5 minutes. Test whether the sweet potatoes are done and simmer longer if necessary.

Turn off the heat under the saucepan, cover, and allow to rest for 20 minutes.

Meanwhile, make the raita by combining all of the ingredients in a medium-sized bowl.

Serve the curry garnished with pumpkin seeds and cilantro leaves along with a dollop of raita, and half a lime for squeezing.

Farmacy Burger

The number one choice on our restaurant menu, so we just couldn't leave it out. This is our plant-based take on the ubiquitous burger. It's full of flavor and nourishing, too. We use black beans to create the delicious taste of the bean burger, supplying protein, magnesium, and vitamins. The other layers are tasty additions that, piled together, create this iconic dish with a heart. It's a winner!

Serves 8

Preparation time: 40 minutes, plus 30 minutes refrigeration and 10 minutes cooking

For the burger

10oz portobello mushrooms

½ cup chopped red bell pepper

3 tablespoons chopped red onion

2 tablespoons brown rice miso

½ cup gluten-free jumbo oat flakes

¼ teaspoon ground black pepper

pinch of salt

¼ teaspoon garlic powder

¼ teaspoon chilli powder

1 tablespoon brown rice flour

1½ tablespoons olive oil

2 cups cooked black beans (*see* page 57)

¾ cup cooked millet (*see* page 51)

¼ cup chopped parsley

To assemble

8 sourdough burger buns

Goji Ketchup (*see* page 112)

1 small Boston or Bibb lettuce

Alioli (*see* page 114)

1 large ripe tomato, sliced

1 jar organic pickles

1 avocado, mashed

Preheat the oven to 350°F.

Put the mushrooms on a baking pan and cook in the oven for 10 minutes. Take them out, drain the juice into a small pitcher, and set both aside to cool.

Put the bell pepper and onion on another baking pan and cook for 15 minutes. Set aside to cool.

Place the cooled vegetables in a food processor and blend. Add the remaining burger ingredients except the millet and parsley and blend again, being careful not to overprocess the mixture or it can turn into a paste.

Finally, add the millet and parsley and stir through.

Cool the mixture in the refrigerator, then take out and shape into 8 individual burgers.

Heat a griddle or skillet over high heat until hot. Cook the burgers until a little crust forms underneath, about 5 minutes, turning once.

Cut the buns in half and toast them if you like. Spoon a tablespoon of goji ketchup onto the surface of the bottom slice of each bun and add a layer of lettuce leaves, followed by a burger. Add a layer of alioli then a slice of tomato and a couple of slices of pickle. Finally, spread mashed avocado on the underside of each bun top and place on top.

Broccoli & Cabbage with Coconut Sauce

This is a beautiful dish of nutrient-loaded vegetables with a gorgeous color which is inspired by a vegetable dish served by Damien Bolger in his Barcelona restaurant. Here we take two ordinary vegetables and combine them in a coconut-based sauce to create a taste sensation. The addition of dill and lime give this dish an herby zing.

Serves 4

Preparation time: 30 minutes plus 20 minutes cooking

For the dill oil

3½oz fresh dill weed

1 cup sunflower or grapeseed oil

1 teaspoon salt

For the cabbage & broccoli

1 head broccoli, cut into florets

¼ cup coconut oil

16 Napa cabbage leaves

2 cups coconut milk

1 tablespoon Philosopher's Sauce (*see* page 64)

squeeze of lime juice

salt and black pepper

To serve

1 cup cooked quinoa (*see* page 51)

dill sprigs

zest of 1 lime

For the dill oil, bring a saucepan of water to a boil and briefly blanch the dill, then remove with a slotted spoon and refresh in a bowl of iced water. (Keep both the boiling and iced water to cook and cool the cabbage in.) Place the dill in a blender with the oil and salt and blend on high for 2 to 3 minutes. Strain off the oil and reserve for later.

In a skillet, sauté the broccoli florets in the coconut oil, allowing them to char a little. While the florets are still al dente, turn the heat off under the pan and allow them to finish cooking as the pan cools. Set aside.

Blanch the cabbage leaves in boiling salted water, then refresh in iced water and drain in a colander.

Pour the coconut milk into a saucepan, bring to a boil, and reduce by half. Add the Philosopher's Sauce and stir. Add the cabbage leaves, the broccoli, a little dill oil, and the lime juice and season with salt and pepper.

Serve with the quinoa, garnished with dill sprigs, lime zest, and some dill oil.

Eggplant Steaks with Tahini & Green Sauce

GF NF VG

These vegetable steaks have a potent flavor and are enhanced by two of our favorite Farmacy sauces—Tahini and Green Sauce. This is a light dish loaded with flavor. Eggplant is a nutrient-packed vegetable that works well served as vegetable steaks, but it can be ruined by cooking it in too much oil. In this recipe, the eggplant is cooked by steaming after being briefly browned in a little oil. It is delicious served with a light salad.

Serves 4

Preparation time: 10 minutes, plus 30 minutes draining

3 firm eggplants, cut into ¾-inch slices
¼ cup olive oil
¼ cup water
salt

To serve

Tahini Sauce (*see* page 68)
Green Sauce (*see* page 66)

Salt the eggplant slices generously to draw out the moisture. This will release any bitterness and reduce the cooking time.

Place the slices vertically in a colander and let stand in the sink for 30 minutes or longer.

When you're ready to cook, take some paper towels and wipe the salt and any moisture from the surface of the slices.

Cook the eggplant slices in 2 batches. Brush half of the slices with 1 tablespoon of olive oil, and heat another tablespoon of oil in a nonstick skillet over high heat. Put the oiled slices in the hot skillet, turning them after 3 minutes. Add 2 tablespoons of water to the pan, cover, and reduce the heat to medium-low for 4 minutes. Repeat with the remaining slices.

Spoon some Tahini Sauce onto a serving plate, place 3 or 4 overlapping eggplant slices over the sauce, and dollop some Green Sauce on top. This dish can be served either warm or cold.

Forager's Pie

A Farmacy stew with a simple, fresh-tasting topping. This dish supplies good levels of fiber and vitamins. Fennel is a great source of calcium, magnesium, and iron and the puréed celery root topping creates a lighter vegan version of a traditional meat pie. Best made with really fresh ingredients.

Serves 4

Preparation time: 20 minutes plus 40 minutes cooking

For the stew

7oz white onion, soaked in cold water for 30 minutes then thinly sliced

⅓ cup olive oil, divided

5 small globe artichokes, peeled, chokes removed, and quartered (*see* Notes below)

1½ tablespoons lemon juice (to be used in preparation of the artichoke hearts)

7oz young fennel bulb, cut into small cubes

1¾oz fresh dill

1lb 2oz asparagus spears, cut into ½-inch pieces

1lb 2oz oyster mushrooms, sliced

½ teaspoon salt

For the celery root

2¼lb celery root, peeled and cut into large cubes

2 tablespoons olive oil

salt

To garnish (optional)

microgreens or sprouts

fennel fronds

Heat a large Dutch oven over medium-low heat and cook the onion in a little of the oil until it becomes translucent. Reduce the heat to cook the onion without coloring it.

Add the artichokes, fennel, and dill and stir well. Cover and cook for 5 minutes, then add 3 tablespoons of water and stir. Cover and cook for another 10 minutes.

At this point the artichokes should be more than half cooked. Add the asparagus spears, mushrooms, and salt and stir. Check the liquid in the pan; there should be a little moisture to continue cooking the vegetables, but if it's dry, add 1 or 2 more tablespoons of water and cover.

Check again after 10 minutes. There should be a little vegetable syrup in the bottom of the pan. If there is too much liquid, strain it off into another saucepan and reduce it before returning it to the vegetables. Cover, remove from the heat, and set aside.

Heat a large saucepan of water until it boils, add the celery root cubes, and cook until tender. Transfer to a food processor with the olive oil and salt to taste. The celery root should have the consistency of mashed potatoes.

Top the cooked vegetables with the celery root and cook under a preheated hot broiler until the pie is warmed through and the topping is golden and crispy.

To serve, spoon onto a plate and garnish with microgreens and fennel fronds, if liked.

Notes

To clean and prepare artichokes, cut them in half and peel back the outer leaves until you can see the tender interior. Clean the fuzz around the artichoke heart and trim away the tougher parts. Dab the remaining heart with lemon juice to prevent oxidation.

Mushrooms & Chard Stems with Tarragon Sauce

GF VG

Serves 4

Preparation time: 20 minutes, plus 15 minutes cooking

For the millet

3 tablespoons lemon juice

⅓ cup olive oil

½ teaspoon salt

3½oz parsley, finely chopped

1 cup cooked millet, cooled (*see* page 51)

For the tarragon sauce

½ cup Cashew Yogurt (*see* page 76)

1 tablespoon pine nuts

1½ tablespoons lemon juice

3 tablespoons tarragon leaves

2 tablespoons olive oil

For the walnut & lime sauce

¾ cup walnuts

3 tablespoons walnut oil

2½oz mixed herbs and some salad leaves (tarragon, parsley, chives, and arugula)

¼ cup lime juice

½ green chile (optional)

For the mushrooms & asparagus

10½oz wild mushrooms

2 tablespoons olive oil, divided

1 garlic clove, minced

8 white asparagus spears, cut into thick matchsticks and tips split

3 tablespoons lemon juice

5½oz Swiss chard stems, cut into sticks (keep the leaves for Farm Green Soup—*see* page 132)

salt

This classic dish was inspired by a walk in the woods. It's a perfect spring or fall supper dish. The recipe is created from a forager's basket of asparagus, mushrooms, and chard stems flavored with tarragon, millet, and nuts. Millet has many nutrients, including calcium, iron, zinc, and magnesium, as well as being a healthy source of essential fats, protein, and fiber. This is a filling dish that looks beautiful. It works well as a dinner party main course and is even better eaten al fresco.

Mix together the lemon juice, oil, and salt to create a dressing for the millet. Mix in the parsley and cold millet and set aside.

Prepare the tarragon sauce by mixing all the ingredients in a blender until smooth.

Prepare the walnut and lime sauce by blending all the ingredients in a food processor until smooth.

Heat a skillet over medium-high heat and sauté the mushrooms in half the olive oil. Move them as little as possible to allow a crust to form. When they are well colored, stir once, add the garlic, swirl for 30 seconds, and set aside. Sauté the asparagus spears in half of the remaining oil until they are al dente. Season with salt and a squeeze of lemon juice and add to the mushrooms.

Next sauté the chard stems in the remaining oil until cooked. A little charring is fine. Season with salt and add to the mushrooms. Toss together until all the elements are combined.

To serve, spoon a scant tablespoon of walnut and lime sauce onto a serving plate and top with the millet and mushroom asparagus mixture and chard. Garnish with generous dollops of tarragon sauce.

Butternut Squash & Spinach Casserole

A hearty casserole with deep flavors, ideal for any season. This dish can be eaten hot in the winter or served deliciously cold in summer. The nuts, squash, and spinach provide vitamins, fiber, zinc, protein, folate, potassium, and other minerals. For this recipe choose a squash with a long neck, which will give you evenly round slices.

Serves 4

Preparation time: 30 minutes, plus soaking and 45 minutes cooking

For the cashew cream

1½ cups raw cashews, soaked for 2 hours, then drained

¼ cup lemon juice

½ teaspoon salt

1 tablespoon nutritional yeast

⅔ cup water

For the squash

neck of 1 large butternut squash, peeled and sliced in disks ¼ inch in thickness

1 tablespoon coconut oil

salt and black pepper

¾ cup crushed macadamia nuts

For the white sauce

2 tablespoons olive oil, plus extra for the dish

7oz spinach

1 garlic clove, minced

½ cup Vegetable Broth (*see* page 60)

½ cup coconut milk

1 tablespoon almond butter

1 teaspoon salt

¼ teaspoon pepper

pinch of grated nutmeg

Place all the ingredients for the cashew cream in a food processor and blend until the mixture has a creamy texture. Add a little more water if needed to create a good consistency. Set aside.

Preheat the oven to 350°F and line 2 cookie sheets with nonstick parchment paper.

Put the squash slices in a bowl and toss with some of the coconut oil. Arrange the squash pieces on the prepared cookie sheets, brush with more coconut oil, and season with salt and pepper. Bake in the oven for 15 minutes or until barely tender. Remove from the oven, but leave the oven on to bake the finished dish.

To make the white sauce, heat the olive oil in a sauté pan and cook the spinach. Remove from the pan and put it on a board to dry. Gently pat the leaves dry if necessary using paper towels; the spinach must be completely dry or it will water down the sauce. Use the same pan to cook the garlic for 1 minute. Add the broth, coconut milk, and almond butter and stir to make a thick sauce. Add the spinach, season with salt, pepper, and nutmeg. Set aside.

Lightly oil a medium-sized, shallow ovenproof dish. Arrange a layer of about 10 overlapping butternut squash pieces on the bottom of the dish, then pour over some cashew cream. Repeat until you have 2 or 3 layers. Cover with the white sauce and sprinkle the macadamia nuts on top.

Cover the casserole with nonstick parchment paper and bake in the oven until heated through; about 10 minutes. Uncover and cook for a further 4 minutes before serving.

The side dishes in this chapter give a blast of taste and color to complement any table. Healthy and nutritious, with style and crunch, these are perfect for sharing and combining with main courses.

Sides

Sweet Potato Home Fries

This recipe offers a healthy alternative to french fries. These delicious home fries provide all the nutritional benefits of the sweet potato, including potassium, dietary fiber, and plenty of vitamin C. Sage and garlic add an Italian touch and the sprout garnish contributes another nutritional layer.

Serves 4

Preparation time: 10 minutes, plus 35 minutes cooking

2¼lb sweet potatoes, cubed
2 tablespoons olive oil, plus a little extra
6 sage leaves, torn into pieces
1 garlic clove, minced
handful of lentil sprouts, to garnish
salt

For the dressing
2 tablespoons olive oil
2 tablespoons apple cider vinegar
¼ teaspoon salt

Put the sweet potatoes into a saucepan of salted boiling water for 3 minutes. Drain and allow to cool slightly.

Heat the olive oil in a skillet until very hot, then add the sweet potato. Sear until a crust begins to form on the potatoes. Reduce the heat to minimum and allow the crust to develop without moving the cubes.

After 5 minutes, check that the heat is low enough not to burn the cubes, but hot enough to continue forming a crust. After 10 minutes, turn the cubes to cook their other sides. Repeat until all sides of the cubes have a crust. Don't move them too often as that prevents a crust from forming.

After 20 minutes, add a little more oil to the skillet along with the sage leaves and toss. After another 5 minutes, add the garlic, and toss again. Remove from the heat.

Make the dressing by combining the ingredients in a screw-top jar, sealing the lid securely, and shaking it vigorously.

Toss the sprouts with the sweet potato cubes and serve with the dressing.

Baked Chickpea Sticks

These chickpea sticks taste as good as they look and their crispness comes from being baked. Chickpeas are high in protein as well as fiber, and, as with all the dishes in the Farmacy kitchen, they are gluten-free and taste divine. The sticks are made from chickpea flour, retaining all the nutrients, and they are a great source of plant-based iron. Fun to eat and great to share, these are perfect as party food or a pre-dinner snack.

Serves 6

Preparation time: 20 minutes, plus 2 hours refrigeration

1¼ cups chickpea flour

2 cups cold water

1 teaspoon salt

1 chile

1 teaspoon Farmacy Seed Mix (*see* page 80)

½ teaspoon lemon zest

¼ teaspoon garlic powder

1 tablespoon olive oil, plus extra for cooking

To garnish (all optional)

sesame seeds

paprika

chopped herbs

Tahini Sauce (*see* page 68)

Blend all the ingredients together in a food processor until smooth. Transfer the contents to a saucepan and cook over low heat, stirring continuously, for about 10 minutes. You will end up with a consistency similar to thick porridge.

Pour into an oiled baking dish and refrigerate until set. This takes about 2 hours.

Preheat the oven to 350°F. Remove the mixture from the dish and cut into chip shapes. Place on an oiled baking pan to prevent them from sticking and bake them for about 30 minutes or until they are golden brown.

Serve sprinkled with sesame seeds, paprika, and chopped fresh herbs, or dip in Tahini Sauce.

Roasted Red Bell Pepper Confit

The smoky sweetness inside red bell peppers is brought out in this recipe, which is high in antioxidants. If your body is in need of some extra iron, try combining bell peppers with your regular iron source as they can significantly help iron absorption. Red bell peppers are also a great source of vitamin B_6, contain more than twice the recommended daily intake of vitamin C, and are known to help increase metabolic rate. This vibrant red dish will add a splash of color to any table. We use this confit in other Farmacy recipes, including the Green Salad with Lentil Dressing (see page 144).

Serves 4 to 6

Preparation time: 5 minutes, plus 40 minutes cooking

1 tablespoon olive oil
3 red bell peppers, cut into strips
1 to 2 red chiles, finely chopped
1 to 2 garlic cloves
1 teaspoon tamari
1 tablespoon sherry vinegar
3 tablespoons water, plus extra if needed
1 tablespoon coconut nectar
salt

Heat the olive oil in a lidded wok. Add the pepper strips. Toss gently until the strips are covered in oil. Sprinkle with a little salt.

After 5 minutes, add the rest of the ingredients and gently toss again. Bring to a boil, reduce the heat, cover, and let simmer. Stir occasionally and then increasingly often as the liquid in the wok disappears.

Make sure the peppers don't stick to the wok. If they are not completely soft, add a little more water and continue to cook. The peppers are ready when they are sweet and tender and all the liquid has evaporated. The whole process takes 30 to 40 minutes.

Roasted Broccoli with Chile & Garlic

A spicy side dish that delivers great taste and lots of nutrients. An easy way to spruce up broccoli and a good source of fiber, protein, iron, calcium, and vitamin C.

Serves 4

Preparation time: 5 minutes, plus 15 minutes roasting

1 head of broccoli, cut into florets
1 to 2 red chiles, minced
1 to 2 garlic cloves, minced
olive oil
2 tablespoons nutritional yeast
salt

Preheat the oven to 375°F.

In a bowl combine all the ingredients except the nutritional yeast. Tip them onto a baking pan and roast them in the oven for about 15 minutes.

Sprinkle with the nutritional yeast and serve

Green Apple & Black Garlic Kimchi

Kimchi is good for the gut and the taste buds and can be made easily at home. It supports the general health of the body and benefits the gut as a result of the fermentation process. Fermented foods are rich in enzymes that support the immune system, help with digestion, and keep the pH of the gut in an optimum balance. The green apple adds a delicious, sharper taste to the mixture when combined with the black garlic, which contributes further health benefits, and creates a great flavor without adding onions.

Serves 8

Preparation time: 1 hour, plus 3 to 5 days fermentation

1 Napa cabbage, about 2¼lb, cut into ¾-inch segments

½ cup salt

3 red chiles, or whatever you have on hand

1 teaspoon grated fresh ginger root

2 black garlic cloves

1 tightly packed tablespoon minced regular garlic

1½ teaspoons coconut nectar

3 tablespoons water

1 green apple, cut into matchsticks

10½oz daikon radish, cut into matchsticks

Add the salt to the cabbage and rub it in to the segments for 5 minutes. Let stand for 1 hour.

Put the cabbage in a colander and rinse 3 times to thoroughly rinse out the salt. Let stand in the colander for 20 minutes.

In a blender, make a paste from the chiles, ginger, black garlic, regular garlic, coconut nectar, and water.

Mix the cabbage, paste, apples, and daikon in a large bowl. Transfer the mixture to a 1½-quart jar with a tight-fitting lid.

Carefully press down the mixture to release any air bubbles and create a snugly packed column. Leave about 1¼ inches of space at the top of the jar and make sure the mixture is completely submerged in the liquid.

Seal the jar loosely (tightly sealed jars could explode when opened) and store in a cool, dry place in a bowl to catch any overflow. Let stand to ferment for 3 to 5 days.

Check the fermentation every day and remove the lid to release air bubbles and any pressure in the jar. Remember to loosely seal the jar again afterwards.

Bok Choy in Yogurt Dressing

This is inspired by a classic Thai bok choy dish. We've added avocado and homemade yogurt to create a creamier, more nutritious and thicker sauce. Bok Choy is a leafy vegetable that has played a large part in Asian cuisine and in traditional Chinese medicine. This dish is a great source of calcium, magnesium, and iron, supplying antioxidants and nutrients to help with strong bones, as well as benefitting heart health and immunity. Bok choy cooks fast, making this light and versatile side quick to put together.

Serves 4
Preparation time: 5 minutes

4 heads of bok choy, shredded
1 ripe avocado, cubed

For the dressing
1 cup coconut or Cashew Yogurt
 (*see* page 76)
2 tablespoons Philosopher's Sauce
 (*see* page 64)
2 tablespoons lime juice, or to taste

To garnish
2 tablespoons crushed roasted peanuts
2 tablespoons black sesame seeds

Put the bok choy in a large heatproof bowl and cover with boiling water. Let stand for a moment, then strain and set aside.

Prepare the dressing by mixing together the yogurt, Philosopher's Sauce, and lime juice. It should taste distinctly of lime, so adjust to taste.

Mix the avocado with the bok choy and the dressing. Top with the crushed peanuts and sesame seeds and serve on a beautiful plate.

Asian Slaw

This light, crunchy slaw can be served alongside a variety of dishes to add color, flavor, and a burst of healthy nutrients including protein, iron, and magnesium. It has an almond butter dressing with not a drop of mayo in sight.

Serves 10

Preparation time: 10 minutes, plus 2 hours chilling

1lb 2oz white cabbage

1 red bell pepper, seeds and core removed

3 carrots

¼ cup rice wine vinegar

¼ cup almond butter

1½ tablespoons lemon juice, plus extra to taste

2 tablespoons coconut nectar

1 teaspoon salt, plus extra for salting

1 teaspoon toasted sesame oil

2 teaspoon tamari

¾ cup coarsely chopped dry-toasted peanuts, to serve

Finely shred the vegetables in a food processor.

Combine the rest of the ingredients except the peanuts in a mixing bowl, stirring until the sauce has a thick texture similar to mayonnaise.

Salt the shredded vegetables, pour the dressing slowly over them, and toss them several times. You want the salad to be well coated, but not drenched, in dressing. Set aside and refrigerate for at least 2 hours before serving.

Add a little lemon juice if needed before serving scattered with the chopped peanuts.

Roasted Cassava & Green Sauce

Cassava is a New World food that's been around for more than 10,000 years. It's a staple food in Brazil, Paraguay, and Indonesia. This vegetable root is loaded with beneficial dietary fiber, which helps reduce blood pressure and cholesterol levels and supports stable blood sugar. It's rich in magnesium, copper, manganese, folate, and vitamin C. All in all, this nutrient-loaded root will help keep you healthy and in good balance.

Serves 4

Preparation time: 5 minutes, plus 35 minutes cooking

2¼lb cassava, peeled, stringy
  center removed, flesh cut
  into sticks ¾ x 4½ inches in size

olive oil

salt

Green Sauce (*see* page 66), to serve

Preheat the oven to 400°F.

Bring a large saucepan of water to a boil, salt the water well, and add the cassava sticks. Cook for about 18 minutes.

Drain and arrange the sticks on a baking pan. Season generously with salt and olive oil and bake until golden; about15 minutes.

Serve with Green Sauce on the side or on the top.

Note
Cassava must be cooked before eating. Never eat it raw.

A selection of naturally delicious desserts. From laid-back sundaes to the best macadamia cookies in the world, there are plenty of sweet things here to fall in love with.

Desserts

Raw Chocolate Tart

This tart is sweetened only with dates. Cacao is known as the food of the gods for good reason. It's packed with antioxidants, high in magnesium and protein and contains many vitamins and minerals. It's also an aphrodisiac and balances hormone swings. The hazelnuts are rich in good fats and support heart, brain, and skin health, making this a naturally mood-enhancing dessert.

Serves 9

Preparation time: 15 minutes, plus 6 hours refrigeration

For the date paste
¾lb Medjool dates, pitted
½ cup water

For the hazelnut crust
⅔ cup hazelnuts
⅓ cup desiccated coconut
3 tablespoons cacao powder
3 tablespoons cacao nibs
pinch of salt
1 cup dates, pitted, plus extra if needed

For the chocolate filling
1⅔ cups cashew nuts, soaked overnight, then drained
10½oz date paste (*see* above)
1 teaspoon vanilla extract
¼ teaspoon salt
1 cup water
1¼ cups cacao powder
½ cup coconut oil

Fruit Chia Jam (*see* page 72), to serve

Start by preparing the date paste. Combine the dates and water in a food processor. Blend until very smooth, scraping down the sides of the processor to make sure the dates are well incorporated. Store in an airtight container in the refrigerator for up to 2 weeks.

To make the crust, put all the ingredients except the dates into a food processor and blend until well combined. Add the dates little by little while blending; the mixture should hold together but be easy to break up. If it is too dry, add more dates. Press the mixture into a 7-inch square springform or loose-bottomed cake pan lined with nonstick parchment paper and put in the refrigerator while you make the filling.

To make the filling, blend together all the ingredients except the cacao powder and coconut oil until smooth. Add the cacao powder and coconut oil and blend until well incorporated. Then pour it evenly onto the crust.

Refrigerate for 6 hours or overnight. If you are short of time you can put the tart in the freezer so that it sets faster. It can also be stored in the freezer for up to 1 month. Try eating it frozen too—it tastes great.

Serve cut into 9 squares topped with Fruit Chia Jam.

Banoffee Pie

This healthy, raw pie is based on one of our classic restaurant desserts. It is a show-stopping dish that's great for a lunch or supper party. This recipe is naturally sweet, sugar-free and nut-free—and made for sharing.

Serves 8

Preparation time: 20 minutes, plus 30 minutes refrigeration and overnight chilling for the coconut cream

For the pie crust

2 cups gluten-free rolled oats

1 cup desiccated coconut

¼ teaspoon vanilla powder

pinch of salt

1 teaspoon lemon juice

½ cup maple syrup, or other sweetener

For the maca caramel sauce

½lb Medjool dates, soaked in warm water for 15 minutes

⅓ cup water

1 teaspoon lemon juice

1 teaspoon maca powder (optional)

3 ripe bananas, cut into ¼-inch slices

cacao nibs, to garnish (optional)

For the coconut whipped cream

2 x 14fl oz cans coconut cream, refrigerated overnight

2 tablespoons raw honey or other sweetener (use a clear sweetener to keep the white color)

1 teaspoon vanilla extract

To make the pie crust, line an 8-inch loose-bottomed tart or flan pan with nonstick parchment paper. Put the oats, coconut, vanilla powder, and salt into a food processor and blend until the mixture has the texture of flour.

Add the lemon juice and maple syrup and blend until combined. Transfer to the lined pan, pressing the mixture down firmly on the bottom and up the sides of the pan using your fingers or the back of a spoon. Let chill in the refrigerator while you make the filling.

For the caramel sauce, place the drained dates in a food processor or blender with the water, lemon juice, and maca powder (if using) and blend until you have a smooth, velvety mixture.

Take the crust out of the freezer and top with the caramel layer. Smooth it down with a spatula or the back of a spoon. Arrange the banana slices on top. Put it back in the refrigerator to chill while you make the cream.

Take the chilled coconut cream cans out of the refrigerator. Carefully scoop the thick layer of solid coconut cream at the top of the cans into a bowl, leaving the liquid behind. Add the honey or other sweetener and the vanilla extract. Use an electric hand mixer to whip the cream until peaks form.

Take the pie out of the refrigerator and top with the whipped coconut cream. You can use a pastry bag to pipe the cream on top or spoon it over the top and spread it out. Sprinkle with cacao nibs on top and serve immediately.

This dish is not suitable for freezing.

Notes

Coconut cream will make a larger quantity of coconut whipped cream than full-fat coconut milk because it contains more cream. It may be firm enough to separate without chilling first, depending on the brand. Only full-fat coconut milk will harden.

Laid-back Sundae

GF VG

Serves 9
**Preparation time: 40 minutes,
plus 5 hours freezing**

1²⁄₃ cups strawberries

For the vanilla ice cream

1¼ cups raw cashews, soaked
(*see* page 49), then drained

½ cup water or unsweetened, nondairy milk

½ cup maple syrup

½ cup unscented coconut oil

2 teaspoons vanilla extract

1 teaspoon raw ground vanilla (or scrape the
seeds from ½ vanilla bean)

½ teaspoon salt

For the chocolate brownie

2 tablespoons ground flaxseed

⅓ cup water

1¾oz chocolate (100 percent cocoa), melted

½ cup coconut oil, plus extra for the pan

½ cup coconut sugar

¼ cup coconut nectar

1 teaspoon vanilla extract

¾ teaspoon gluten-free baking powder

pinch of salt

½ cup cacao powder

½ cup buckwheat flour

⅓ cup rice flour

¼ cup ground almonds (or tigernut
flour for nut-free version)

⅓ cup chocolate chips

For the caramelized pecans

½ cup pecans

1½ tablespoons maple syrup

For the caramel sauce

3½ tablespoons coconut butter (from
the bottom of the jar, rather than
the oily top layer)

½ cup maple syrup

2 tablespoons coconut oil

½ teaspoon vanilla extract

"OMG!" is the usual exclamation when people first taste this. Vanilla is a truly medicinal food that has been used for centuries. It enhances brain health and mood, as well as being a great source of magnesium, potassium, and calcium as *well* as being an aphrodisiac. This recipe contains no refined sugars, can be nut-free, and uses ground flaxseed instead of eggs.

Place the ice cream ingredients in a blender and blend until smooth. Transfer to a freezer-proof container and freeze for 5 to 6 hours or overnight.

Next make the brownies. Preheat the oven to 350°F. Lightly oil a 7-inch square cake pan and line it with nonstick parchment paper. Mix the flaxseed and water in a bowl. Set aside for 15 minutes.

Melt the chocolate and coconut oil in a heatproof bowl over a saucepan of boiling water. Scrape into a large bowl with the coconut sugar, nectar, and vanilla extract. Beat to combine. Add the flaxseeds and beat again. Then add the baking powder, salt, and cacao powder and beat once more.

Add the flours and almond meal or tigernut flour and fold in with a spatula until just mixed. Then add the chocolate chips.

Pour the batter into the prepared pan and bake for 20 minutes or until the edges appear dry and slightly fluffy and the center is no longer wet. Remove from the oven and let cool in the pan for 15 minutes before gently lifting out. Once cool, slice into squares.

While the brownies are cooking, prepare the pecans by coating them in maple syrup. Place them on a cookie sheet lined with nonstick parchment paper and bake in the oven for 10 minutes until toasted. Take out and set aside to cool.

For the sauce, melt the coconut butter in a heatproof bowl over a saucepan of boiling water. Add the maple syrup, coconut oil, and vanilla and stir well to combine, then set aside.

To assemble, place a spoonful of sauce in each bowl, top with cubes of brownie, scoops of ice cream, some caramelized pecans, and strawberries. Drizzle with more caramel sauce and serve.

The brownies will stay fresh in an airtight container for up to 3 days and will keep in the freezer for up to 1 month. Pour any leftover caramel sauce into molds and put into the refrigerator to set into coconut fudge.

DESSERTS 219

White Macadamia Cookies

These cookies are delicious at any time of the day. Macadamia nuts are high in vitamin A, iron, and protein. The cookies are free from refined sugar and grains, and are also paleo-friendly. The only problem will be eating just one! We love them dipped in a nut-milk drink or as a cozy evening snack when watching a movie. They are crumbly and so delicious that it's hard to stop eating them.

Makes 16
Preparation time: 30 minutes

1½ tablespoons chia seeds
¼ cup water
1½ cups ground almonds
½ cup coconut flour
¾ cup coconut sugar
½ cup cashew butter (or other
    nut butter)
½ cup coconut oil
2 teaspoons gluten-free baking powder
1 tablespoon vanilla extract
pinch of salt
3 tablespoons macadamia nuts
½ cup vegan white chocolate chips

Mix the chia seeds with the water. Let stand for 5 to 10 minutes until the seeds have absorbed all the water and are gelatinous.

Put all the other ingredients except the nuts and chocolate chips into a food processor. Whizz together until well combined. Add the nuts and chocolate chips and mix them in with a wooden spoon until well dispersed.

Use an ice cream scoop to measure out balls of cookie dough, placing them on a baking pan lined with nonstick parchment paper and flattening them with your hands into cookie shapes. Put the pan in the refrigerator. When the cookies are completely set and cold, preheat the oven to 350°F.

Bake the chilled cookies for 15 minutes until golden. They will feel a little soft when you take them out of the oven but will harden as they cool.

Let the cookies sit for 5 minutes to cool and harden, then transfer them to a cooling rack until completely cold.

Matcha Lime Avocado Cakes

GF NF R VG

A creamy and light combination of matcha, lime, and avocado blended together to create a zingy taste sensation, these nut-free cakes are full of healthy fats and proteins. Pumpkin seeds are an excellent source of magnesium and zinc, helping to support the heart and immune system. The matcha supplies good levels of antioxidants, as well as working as a metabolism booster. This is a great dessert to share, bringing color and healthy flavors to the table.

Serves 4

Preparation time: 15 minutes, plus 5 hours freezing

For the crust

¾ cup raw pumpkin seeds
4 soft Medjool dates, pitted
½ tablespoon coconut oil

For the matcha filling

I avocado, pitted
¼ cup lime juice
¼ cup maple syrup
1 tablespoon coconut oil
zest of 1 lime
1 teaspoon vanilla extract
1 tablespoon matcha powder
¼ cup full-fat coconut milk
pinch of salt

To serve

⅔ cup coconut yogurt
matcha powder, for sprinkling
1 lime, thinly sliced

Put all the crust ingredients into a food processor and blend into a fine, sticky mixture similar to unbaked streusel topping. Split this mixture between 4 round molds (or 4 holes of a muffin pan) and press to form a flat, even crust. Put the molds or muffin pan in the freezer while you make the filling.

Put all the filling ingredients into a blender and whizz at high speed until smooth. Take the molds out of the freezer and spoon the mixture onto the prepared crusts, smoothing out the tops.

Return to the freezer for at least 3 hours, or overnight, to set. If frozen overnight, take the molds out of the freezer about 1 hour before serving.

Serve with a dollop of coconut yogurt, a sprinkling of sifted matcha powder, and lime slices.

Fig Tarte Tatin

When we were testing recipes for this book, our friend Paul came to the house carrying a basket of figs fresh from the tree. Being a warm and friendly team, we happily accepted his offer to make us a dessert. When we first tasted his tarte, we knew the recipe had to be in the book. Once you've tried it, you'll be hooked, too. Figs are a rich source of minerals, including magnesium and calcium, and are also powerful antioxidants. This is a delicious dessert with no refined sugar or gluten—a summer delight.

Serves 12
Preparation time: 50 minutes

For the crust
1½ cups buckwheat flour, plus a little extra for rolling out
¾ cup ground almonds
½ cup coconut sugar
1 tablespoon ground flaxseed
2½ tablespoons water
⅓ cup coconut butter
3 to 4 tablespoons almond milk
zest of 1 lemon
pinch of salt

For the topping
1 tablespoon coconut butter
2 tablespoons coconut sugar
1lb figs, quartered

For the coconut cream
14fl oz can full-fat coconut milk
1 tablespoon honey or other sweetener
½ teaspoon vanilla extract

Preheat the oven to 350°F.

To make the crust, put the buckwheat flour and ground almonds into a bowl with the coconut sugar and stir until combined. Mix the flaxseed with the water and add to the bowl along with the coconut butter, then slowly pour in the almond milk. Stir until the mixture has a doughy consistency. Cover the bowl with a clean dish cloth and place it in the refrigerator for 30 minutes.

Next, make the topping. Smear a round 12-inch dish (ideally a clay dish) with the coconut butter. Pour the coconut sugar evenly over the coconut butter. Arrange the figs evenly over the bottom.

Spread a little buckwheat flour over a clean surface and roll out the dough until it is about ⅓-inch thick and a little larger than the dish. Slice the dough into quarters and place the quarters on top of the figs until they are all covered. Once you've covered the figs, smooth the pastry quarters into one another and tuck the edges down the side of the dish.

Place in the oven and cook for 30 minutes until golden brown on top. When you are ready to serve, place a plate on top of the dish. Holding them together firmly, turn the dish and plate upside down so the figs are on top, and the tarte is sitting on the plate. Gently lift the dish off of the plate.

Make the coconut cream by blending all the ingredients together until well combined.

To serve, cut into 12 slices and drizzle each with coconut cream.

Pitaya Tart

This is the prettiest pink tart we've ever seen. Pitaya is also known as dragon fruit. It is loaded with nutrients, including vitamin C, calcium, and phytonutrients and is also rich in antioxidants. This raw, intensely colorful tart is quick to make and will look stunning on your table.

Serves 12

**Preparation time: 15 minutes, plus
   5 hours freezing**

For the crust

1 cup almonds

6 dates

½ cup coconut flour

¼ teaspoon vanilla powder

2 tablespoons coconut oil, melted

pinch of salt

For the filling

2 cups cashews, soaked (*see* page 49)

7oz frozen pitaya

1½ teaspoons lemon juice

¼ cup maple syrup

½ teaspoon vanilla extract

pinch of salt

2 tablespoons coconut oil, melted

blackberries and blueberries, to serve

To make the crust, put the nuts and the dates in a food processor and blend until they are broken down and combined. Add the rest of the crust ingredients and process until well combined.

Line an 8-inch round tart or flan pan with nonstick parchment paper and fill it with the crust, pressing it down to form an even layer over the bottom and up the sides. Put it in the freezer while you prepare the filling.

For the filling, rinse the cashews and drain them well. Put in a blender with all the other ingredients except the coconut oil. Blend until you have a smooth consistency. Then slowly pour in the coconut oil, still blending.

Take the tart pan out of the freezer and pour the filling evenly over the crust. Return to the freezer for about 3 hours, until set.

Take the tart out of the freezer and defrost for 20 minutes at room temperature (or 1 hour in the refrigerator) before serving with the purple berries.

This will keep in the freezer for up to 1 month.

Chocolate Wheels

GF R VG

Makes 20
Preparation time: 40 minutes,
  plus 30 minutes refrigeration

5½oz Raspberry Chia Jam (*see* page 72)

For the cookie
1 cup shredded coconut
¾ cup ground almonds
½ cup cashews or macadamia nuts
2 tablespoons coconut butter
¼ cup maple syrup
½ teaspoon vanilla powder

For the coconut marshmallow
¼ cup coconut butter
3 tablespoons liquid coconut oil
⅓ cup coconut cream, or fat from
  the top of a can of full-fat coconut
  milk chilled overnight
½ teaspoon vanilla extract
1½ tablespoons maple syrup

For the chocolate coating
3 tablespoons cacao butter
½ cup cacao powder
¼ cup liquid coconut oil
2½ tablespoons maple syrup
Alternatively, melt 5½oz dairy-free dark
  chocolate (72 percent cocoa) if you don't
  want to make the chocolate yourself

These Chocolate Wheels have a healthy edge. They taste gorgeous, with layers of fruity chia jam, coconut marshmallow, and cacao chocolate. Grown-up kids and real kids love these. They are great for parties, snacks, and to share from a lunchbox. You will need a 2½-inch round cookie cutter for this recipe.

To prepare the cookie, put the shredded coconut, ground almonds, and cashews or macadamia nuts into a food processor and pulse until you have a fine texture. Soften the coconut butter by putting the jar in hot water, then add 2 tablespoons to the food processor, along with the maple syrup and vanilla powder, and pulse until well combined.

Turn out the mixture and form it into a ball, then roll out on nonstick parchment paper until it is about ½ inch thick. Cut out the cookies using a round cookie cutter until you have used up all the dough. Put on a cookie sheet and place in the freezer while you make the other components.

For the coconut marshmallow, put all the ingredients in a blender and whizz until smooth and creamy. Place in the refrigerator for 10 minutes.

To make the chocolate coating, melt the cacao butter in a heatproof bowl over a saucepan of boiling water. Add the other ingredients and stir together until smooth and silky. Alternatively, if you are using store-bought chocolate, melt the chocolate.

To assemble, spread a layer of marshmallow on one of the cookies, followed by a layer of jam. Top with another cookie, sandwiching the layers together. Repeat until you have used all the cookies.

Using 2 forks dunk each cookie sandwich into the bowl of melted chocolate to coat, then place on a cookie sheet lined with nonstick parchment paper. Put in the refrigerator for 30 minutes until the chocolate is set.

These cookies will last for 10 days in an airtight container in the refrigerator. They can be frozen for up to a month. When frozen, remove from the freezer 10 minutes before eating, to allow them to soften slightly.

Chocolate & Almond Nice Cream

Regulars at Farmacy know we love a nice cream. It was hard to choose which flavor to include. Emily loves this banana and almond version and could quite happily eat it every day. It has a creamy edge and chocolate fudge chunks in the middle. There are no grains in the recipe and no flour, and it is sweetened with natural sugars. All the ingredients support good health. This is a nice cream your body won't mind you eating.

Serves 6 to 8 servings

Preparation time: 15 minutes, plus 4 hours freezing

For the fudge

¾ cup coconut flour

3 tablespoons cacao powder

⅓ cup maple syrup

¾ teaspoon vanilla extract

pinch of salt

For the ice cream

6 peeled, sliced, and frozen bananas (you can use fresh but these take longer to set)

¾ cup smooth Almond Butter (*see* page 74)

3 tablespoons maple syrup

1 teaspoon vanilla extract

Put all the fudge ingredients into a small food processor and blend until well combined. The mixture should resemble dry brownie pieces. Turn into a bowl and break up the mixture into chunks or finer pieces, if desired.

Put all the ice cream ingredients into a blender and whizz at a high speed until completely smooth. Transfer the mixture into a freezer-proof container. Add the fudge pieces, folding them in with a spoon until they are evenly distributed. Freeze for 4 to 5 hours until set.

Here are some of our favorite natural recipes for keeping your home and body healthy without using chemicals or toxic ingredients. We use natural ingredients in these home and beauty preparations. Ditch store-bought products in favor of those you make at home, so you can be sure they are chemical-free and organic; good for you, good for your wallet, and kind to the planet.

Home & Beauty

Body Beautiful Scrub

This easy recipe uses natural ingredients to exfoliate the skin and keep it glowing and healthy. You can use it daily, or weekly for a more intense scrub. It's homemade, so you can be sure there are no chemicals or nasties in there.

Makes 1 cup
Preparation time: 5 minutes

½ cup granulated sugar (we use coconut sugar)

½ cup coconut oil

1 teaspoon vanilla powder, or your favorite essential oil (optional)

Combine all the ingredients and put in a glass container with a lid. Seal and store. It will lasts for months in a cool place.

How to use

Rub gently on your skin while in the shower. Massage and rinse.

Edible Body Butter

We love using natural ingredients like these to keep skin glowing, smooth, and healthy. Skin is the biggest organ of the body and it doesn't help to cover it in chemicals. Love your body; use natural preparations. You can eat this, too. It's a versatile and fun-to-use body butter.

Makes 2 cups
Preparation time: 15 minutes

1 cup cacao butter
1 cup coconut oil
a few drops of your favorite essential oil, such as rose (optional)

Put the cacao butter and coconut oil in a heatproof glass dish over a bowl of hot water to melt. Once melted, mix with any oil you like. Pour into a beautiful container.

Lasts for 3 months sealed and stored in a cool place.

How to use

Apply to the whole body for wonderful hydration and moisture.

Body beautiful scrub

Edible body butter

Natural body wash

Oat & honey
face cleanser

Natural Body Wash

Cleansers are important because we put them on our skin every day. Many body washes are loaded with chemicals. Castile soap is a pure, natural, plant-based soap that is gentle on the skin. It is one of the best biodegradable soaps that can be made by hand. This recipe gives you a pure and safe body wash to keep your skin clean and looking healthy and radiant.

Makes 3 cups
Preparation time: 5 minutes

¼ cup liquid Castile soap
3 cups water
3 tablespoons oatmeal
3 drops tea tree oil
3 drops peppermint essential oil

Mix all the ingredients together and store sealed in a screw-top jar.

Oat & Honey Face Cleanser

Here's a simple, natural recipe for cleansing your skin, leaving it feeling fresh and cared for. Many over-the-counter cleansers are loaded with preservatives and strong ingredients that we don't want to use on the face. This cleanser is made with oats, which are anti-inflammatory, and perfect for all skin types, including sensitive skins. Honey is antibacterial, full of antioxidants, and helps nourish and cleanse the skin.

Makes ½ cup
Preparation time: 15 minutes

¼ cup rolled oats

2 tablespoons honey

2 tablespoons sweet almond, coconut, or olive oil, plus extra if needed

Grind the rolled oats in a coffee grinder, blender, or food processor until soft and powdery.

Transfer the powder to a bowl and mix with the rest of the ingredients until you have a thick, sticky mixture. If it's too sticky or clumpy, add a little extra oil.

Store sealed in an airtight container.

How to use

Wet your face with warm water. Place a small amount (less than 1 teaspoon) of the mixture in your hands and rub them together. Massage the mixture onto your skin in a circular motion, rubbing gently for a couple of minutes. You can leave this on for 5 to 10 minutes for deep pore cleansing. Wash off with warm water and pat your skin dry.

Detox Face Mask

From time to time, everyone's face can use a little extra loving care. This is our go-to recipe for a great face mask treatment containing only pure and natural ingredients. You can use this weekly or whenever you feel you need a beauty boost. The clay and charcoal naturally draw out impurities from the skin. The honey has antibacterial properties and chlorella helps promote cell regeneration and brightens the complexion. You can buy clay, charcoal powder, and chlorella online or from health food stores.

Makes 2 face masks
Preparation time: 5 minutes

2 teaspoons water
1 teaspoon bentonite clay
1 teaspoon activated charcoal powder
¼ teaspoon chlorella powder
½ teaspoon raw honey

Put the water into a small glass bowl and sprinkle the clay over the top. Allow the clay to absorb the water for about 10 seconds, then add the other ingredients. This makes the mixture easier to combine.

Use a small rubber spatula to mash and mix everything together. You may need to mix for a few minutes to remove lumps from the clay.

This mask doesn't store well because there are no preservatives.

How to use

Apply the mask liberally to your face. Allow to dry for about 10 minutes before washing off with warm water.

Fresh Breath Rinse

This mouth rinse helps care for teeth and gums, as well as supporting the remineralization of teeth. It's also effective in helping reduce inflammation or irritation of the gums and teeth. Salt water helps keep the mouth healthy and neutralizes the pH (acidity) of saliva. Use this every day to help keep your mouth, gums, and teeth in great shape.

Makes 2 cups
Preparation time: 5 minutes

4 teaspoons pure salt, such as Himalayan or Celtic
2 cups boiling water
2 drops food grade peppermint essential oil

Place the salt in a glass jar with a screw-top lid and pour the water over it. Add the peppermint oil.

Put the lid on the jar securely and shake it to dissolve some of the salt. It will dissolve further over a few days.

Lasts for 1 month sealed and stored in a cool place.

How to use

Use before and after brushing your teeth. Take a mouthful, swish it around your mouth and spit it out. Do not swallow.

Natural Toothpaste

VG

This is a natural alternative to commercial toothpastes without harmful ingredients. Some brands use fluoride in toothpaste, which is highly toxic; avoid these. Check the ingredients in your toothpaste carefully. Better still, make your own so you know exactly what's in it. This recipe has natural cleansing power. The coconut oil helps get rid of toxins and keep teeth naturally white and clean as well as being antibacterial and antimicrobial. Baking soda neutralizes the acid-loving bacteria in your mouth, which are responsible for causing cavities. It also helps whiten teeth, remove plaque, and maintain healthy gums. Peppermint oil is also antibacterial.

Makes about ¼ cup
Preparation time: 5 minutes

¼ cup coconut oil, preferably unscented

1½ tablespoons baking soda

10 to 15 drops food grade peppermint essential oil

5 drops myrrh extract (optional)

2 drops liquid stevia, to sweeten (optional)

Put the coconut oil in a small saucepan and soften it over low heat. Remove from the heat and let cool slightly. Mix in the other ingredients and stir well.

Once the mixture has solidified, give it another stir, as the baking soda may have settled at the bottom.

Store in a glass jar and seal with a lid. Lasts for 3 months in a sealed jar in a cool place.

How to use

Use twice daily on a wet toothbrush for healthy and clean teeth and mouth.

Love Earth Home Cleaner

VG

House-cleaning products can be quite toxic, especially those that contain perfumes, strong chemicals, and bleach. This is a recipe for an all-purpose cleaner you can use to clean surfaces and remove water deposit stains on shower panels, chrome bathroom fittings, windows, bathroom mirrors, and so on. It's a versatile cleaner that causes no harm but keeps your house fresh and free of toxic sprays and harsh chemical agents. You will need a spray bottle to store it in.

Makes about 2 quarts
Preparation time: 5 minutes

½ cup apple cider vinegar
¼ cup baking soda
2 quarts water
juice of 1 lemon

Mix all the ingredients together and pour into a spray bottle.

Index

(page numbers in *italics* refer to photographs)

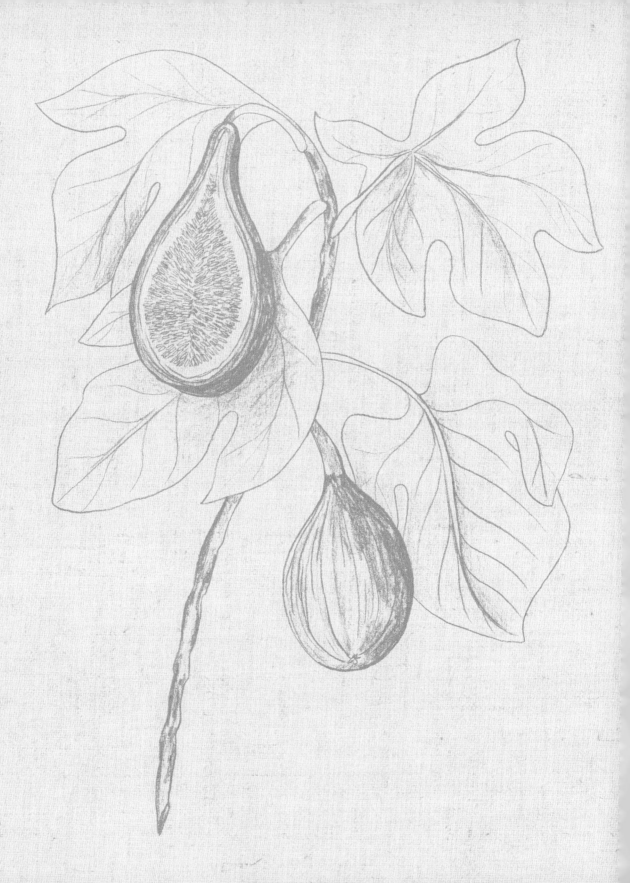

Cookery Notes

Key to nutritional information recipe codes:
GF = gluten free
NF = nut free
R = raw
VG = vegan

Standard level spoon measurements are used in all recipes.

Fresh herbs should be used unless otherwise stated.

Ovens should be preheated to the specific temperature. If using
a convection oven, follow manufacturer's instructions for adjusting
the time and the temperature.

Salt should be sea salt flakes unless otherwise stated. See page 41
for more on salt.

Pepper should be freshly ground black pepper unless otherwise stated.

Honey should be raw and can be substituted in any recipes for coconut
nectar or maple syrup to keep it vegan.

All nuts should be raw and unsalted, unless stated otherwise.

Water should always be filtered.

This book includes dishes made with nuts and nut derivatives.
It is advisable for those with known allergic reactions to nuts and
nut derivatives and those who may be potentially vulnerable to these
allergies, such as pregnant and nursing mothers, older people, babies,
and young children, to avoid dishes made with nuts and nut oils.
It is also prudent to check the labels of pre-prepared ingredients
for the possible inclusion of nut derivatives.

We regularly update our website with details of stockists that may help
you when it comes to sourcing some of the more unusual ingredients
used in our recipes.

Acknowledgments

The Farmacy team have worked together combining their skills and knowledge to create a new vision for plant-based food. This collaboration of understanding comes from many years of discovery in eating and living consciously.

We would like to extend a heartfelt thank you to everyone who has been a part of the creative process, allowing us to bring health and happiness to your kitchen.

The team gives thanks to Camilla Fayed for leading the way with her vision for Farmacy and the first Farmacy recipe book. Camilla and Susie Pearl worked closely to bring the concept of Farmacy Kitchen from an idea into this beautiful book, along with the great food team.

Thanks to Pietro Cuevas and Emily Pearson for creating delicious food combinations and innovative recipes. Thanks to Emma Newman for being the backbone of the project, whose invaluable assistance enabled us to bring this book to life.